Teaching Psychotherapy
of Psychotic Patients

DAN H. BUIE, Jr., M.D.: Psychiatrist, New England Medical Center Hospitals, Boston, and Assistant Professor of Psychiatry, Tufts University School of Medicine.

JOHN T. MALTSBERGER, M.D.: Associate Director of Psychiatry, Massachusetts Mental Health Center, Boston, and Instructor in Psychiatry, Harvard Medical School.

ELVIN V. SEMRAD, M.D.: Director of Psychiatry, Massachusetts Mental Health Center, Boston, and Professor of Psychiatry, Harvard Medical School.

JULIUS SILBERGER, Jr., M.D.: Associate Director, Southard Clinic, Massachusetts Mental Health Center, Boston, and Instructor in Psychiatry, Harvard Medical School.

DAVID VAN BUSKIRK, M.D.: Director, South Shore Mental Health Center, Quincy, Massachusetts, and Assistant Clinical Professor of Psychiatry, Tufts University School of Medicine.

Teaching Psychotherapy
of Psychotic Patients

Supervision of Beginning Residents
in the "Clinical Approach"

By: ELVIN V. SEMRAD, M.D.

Editor: DAVID VAN BUSKIRK, M.D.

Workshop Collaborators:

DAN H. BUIE, JR., M.D.

JOHN T. MALTSBERGER, M.D.

ELVIN V. SEMRAD, M.D.

JULIUS SILBERGER, JR., M.D.

DAVID VAN BUSKIRK, M.D.

Grune & Stratton   New York and London

Library of Congress Catalog No. 69-15738

Printed in the U.S.A.
(G-B)

To generations of residents
who have taught us
even as they began their careers

Foreword

A student's first planned intervention intended to modify the mental and physical behavior of another human is often a troubling encounter. Most are prepared for the patient's symptoms but many students are disturbed by their own reactions to the situation. The process of learning that the subtle interplay between the psychologic processes of the therapist and the patient is the most important element in therapy requires reorientation of the conventional concept of the doctor-patient relationship. The most effective method of teaching psychotherapy is a modification of the therapeutic situation in which the neophyte discusses his therapeutic maneuvers and the patients' and his own reactions to them with a more experienced therapist. This latter experience is called "supervision," but it is in fact a dual situation in which the supervisor and the therapist examine the therapeutic interaction between the patient and the therapist and give tacit if not overt attention to the interaction between therapist and supervisor.

Problems in supervision seldom arise in examining the theoretical aspects of the patient's problems, or in arriving at a preliminary course of action with therapeutic intent. The problems arise when the supervisor attempts to aid the therapist in managing his reactions to the patient, but does so without recognition that this is in fact a form of limited goal therapy of the supervisee, and that supervision is subject to all the nuances of therapy including transference, countertransference, role expectations, adjustments to differing cultural backgrounds, etc.

Teaching and learning is a never ending process (or should be) for all of us and the meaningful material for this education proceeds from patient to therapist to supervisor and back. The authors of this monograph have attempted to discuss the processes involved and to provide some guidelines for the supervisor. That this is a highly individual process is amply illustrated by the variations in content, writing style, and apparent life style of the authors. The supervisor reading this should accept it as a marine chart or map from which he may be helped to chart a course for his own teaching rather than a subway map which if followed compulsively will get him certainly to a given destination.

JACK R. EWALT, M.D.

Contents

Introduction

The process of becoming a therapist for psychotic patients as experienced by the beginning psychiatric resident is part of a poorly understood transition which several supervisors have studied at the Massachusetts Mental Health Center. On arriving in a complicated psychiatric hospital, a physician is confronted with a host of novel and stressing demands and institutions, and his subsequent professional career will be obviously affected by the course of events at the outset of his training. Traditionally, the supervising psychiatrist has been a central figure in the education of residents, but there has been little consensus as to what role he plays in the constellation of social and psychological forces encountered by the developing professional. This monograph is an attempt to explore the problems first-year residents encounter and the importance of supervision in their resolutions as evolved in a major teaching center where residents are supervised in the therapy of psychotic patients from the outset of their training.

Our rationale in setting the treatment of psychotic patients at the start of a physician's experience with psychiatry has far more than historical precedent behind it. Steps involved in learning to be a psychotherapist rest on an early familiarization with unconscious processes and with ego defenses. We have found that psychotic regressions offer singular opportunities for the observation of undisguised primitive drives and the concurrent ego fragmentation and restitution. Overwhelming affects are at the crux of major mental illness, and the beginner encounters personality disintegration where the stresses of reality led to unbearable feelings. In a sense, we capitalize on the obviousness of the psychotic pathology as we attempt to convey a unitary theory of mental functioning and mental impair-

1

ment, the sickest patients being at the extreme of the continuum using narcissistic defenses to a much greater degree than neurotic individuals. Residents find the transition from treatment of the hospitalized physically ill to treatment of the hospitalized mentally ill less difficult since in our hospital they find a continuity of many medical institutions and practices including the use of nursing and occupational therapy personnel, concern with the dependency expectations of patients, use of medication, and staff rounds.

The literature concerning supervision of psychotherapy has been valuable to us as stimulating several directions of interest. In particular, Ekstein and Wallerstein* have extensively discussed supervision as carried on at The Menninger Foundation and have demonstrated parallel patterns in learning problems among psychologists, somewhat sophisticated psychiatrists, and uncertain beginners. D'Zuma† has dealt with the general question of supervising residents without stressing the importance of the beginner's anxiety to the growth process. Most of what has been wriien about supervision has concerned psychotherapy or psychoanalysis of better integrated patients by somewhat experienced therapists. Much of this theoretical framework is germane to our interests, but there are many aspects brought into focus by our work which have been previously overlooked. The introduction of the beginning resident to the psychotherapy of psychotic patients poses unique problems.

This monograph is the product of a small workshop consisting of four young and one senior supervisor, which has been meeting over a period of 4 years. At these meetings we have exchanged illustrative experiences, have followed inten-

---

* Ekstein, Rudolf and Wallerstein, R. S.: *The Teaching and Learning of Psychotherapy.* New York. Basic Books, 1958.

† T. L. D'Zuma, The function of individual supervision. In: Hoffman, F. H. (Ed.): *Teaching of Psychotherapy,* International Psychiatric Clinics, Vol. I, #2, April 1964, pp. 377–387.

sively the supervisory data of some residents, and have gradually evolved working conceptualizations of the supervisory process and its impact on professional growth. The younger supervisors are within 7 to 9 years of the beginning of their own residency, having trained at this same hospital with the senior member who was a dominant influence in their development. All members of the group are actively committed to psychoanalytic training. Since they are sensitive to their own inexperience, these young supervisors are in a position to feel vulnerable to and immediately attentive to the institutional and emotional influences affecting all people who enter our field.

It is our purpose to present an integrated approach to the teaching of a particular form of treatment (psychodynamic psychotherapy) of a certain group of patients (hospitalized and psychotic persons) at the beginning of the training of the psychiatrist at the Massachusetts Mental Health Center. Thus we have greatly narrowed our field, yet we encourage the general application of our findings. The concept of empathy, the nature of interpersonal needs, and the vicissitudes of aggressive identification are each seen very clearly in supervision as we describe it, but are also found of equal importance in many aspects of the work and training of the psychodynamic psychiatrist.

We wish to express our appreciation to Miss Rose Miscio, Miss Virginia Egan, and Mrs. Melvia Sears for the transcribing of tapescripts and manuscripts and to Miss Susan Payne for her assistance with our bibliography.

Elvin V. Semrad, M.D.
David Van Buskirk, M.D.

CHAPTER I

Teaching the Clinical Approach

By Elvin V. Semrad, M.D.

In our work, we use the term *clinical approach* to emphasize that the science we are teaching is grounded in a setting of doctor-patient relationships. *Psychodynamic psychiatry*[1] is the discipline to which we belong, and we subsume within that speciality many assumptions and commonly held convictions which bear on the nature of mental illness in general and on psychoses specifically. In fact, we presume a *science of psychodynamics* which can be traced as it has grown and is evolving towards the understanding of forces within people which operate to produce symptoms, affects, or behaviors. The trained therapist discovers these forces in his investigations and once he places them in perspective, he has ways in which he may influence their interaction. It is only in recent decades that major training centers committed to such an approach have developed. Controversy remains and we welcome its role in fostering new insights.

4

HISTORICAL ROOTS OF PSYCHODYNAMIC PSYCHIATRY

A grasp of our professional situation as teachers, clinicians, and scientists relies upon a background of historical precedents which deserve focus. The earliest documented inclinations towards our current point of view on mental illness are found in Greek thought. Plato and Hippocrates each rejected demoniacal possession as explanations of depressions, upsets, or seizures. Their naturalistic and humanitarian views surfaced briefly 400 years before Christ, but the abuses of subsequent centuries demonstrate how readily man has called in external agents to explain the derangements of the mind. There was occasional recognition of more humane approaches by such Roman physicians as Soranus and Caelius Aurelianus (ca. 100 A.D.) who wrote with feeling of the crazed person's need for human warmth and protection. But systematic investigation, treatment, or even respect for withdrawn, hallucinated, or maniacal people was rare during the years between the deterioration of Rome and the Reformation. Fear produced spiritistic explanations for insanity, and during these Dark Ages needs to control the irrational led to extreme punishments such as persisted in the hanging of witches in our own country. The Renaissance replaced dogmatic tradition by scientism and skepticism and such persons as Johann Weyer (1515–1588) and Philippus Paracelsus (1493–1541) protested the brutality of their contemporaries. Until 200 years ago, there had been only a few recorded voices willing to recognize qualities in the insane common to the minds of all men, and these voices had been brief or weak with little impact on cultures searching for supernatural forces to explain the experience of man on earth.

The intellectual revolution of the eighteenth century brought new attention to the problems of the insane. Scientific curiosity became interwoven with a feeling for the human needs of these abused persons. In France, Philippe Pinel unlocked the chains of the Bicetre. Jean Esquirol groped for classification of mental symptoms. In England, William Tuke befriended the ostracized, and in our own country, Benjamin Rush devised his tranquilizer chair which gave a semblance of gentleness to restraint, although in this instance we still detect some rationalized sadism. But the academic and Germanic systemization leading to Kraepelinian concepts of dementia pracox which are the end product of nineteenth century intellectualism reveal the inherent limitations of pure reason. Failures to grasp the significance of feelings particularly as forces operating outside awareness confounded these physicians, led to their therapeutic nihilism, and diverted their interests to organic factors.

"Moral" treatment was developed in America by such men as Pliny Earle, Amariah Brigham, and Samuel Woodward. It aimed at the arousal of the dormant faculties of the mind through communal life in mental hospitals. According to these fundamentally humane precepts, patients were required to invest interests in activities outside themselves, cooperating with others in manual, intellectual, recreational, or religious directions. The sharing of experiences both in groups and individually had a positive effect on many patients, but the theoretical or scientific considerations were minor. This was a pragmatic American approach.

Adolph Meyer brought several of these streams of thought to a synthesis in his psychobiology. His commitment was to the patient as a person whose life was in a state of disequilibrium and required re-education from the psychiatrist. His science depended on integration of personal, social, and biological data which he individualized for each patient. But the forces he included in his therapeutics were mostly inherited, social, and behavioral. Harry Stack Sullivan's investigation of interpersonal forces has of course carried these considerations much nearer to our conceptions.

The contributions of Freud and of subsequent psychoanalytic practitioners are central to the continuing development of psychodynamic psychiatry. The role of early childhood and family relations, the conceptualization of the unconscious, the place of sexuality and aggression, the operation of various mental mechanisms, the phenomenology of conflict, anxiety, and guilt, and the somatic language of emotions were rapidly delineated during the last 75 years. Psychoanalysis is a most important instrument for obtaining data pertinent to the operations of psychic energy. Theoretical insights from such information obtained on the couch become broadly applicable to the understanding of psychiatric maladjustment and human relationships. By making choices more rational and goal-directed, the science of psychoanalysis permits the psychiatrist to be increasingly scientific and less blindly guided by humanitarian ideals.[2] Thus, the impact of analysis had been to extend the science originally developed by Meyer, making it holistic by providing genetic, dynamic, economic, and structural as well as adaptive points of view.

The essence of mental illness is consistent and persistent. Today we describe it in approximate terms when we speak of an ego overwhelmed by the vicissitudes of life. The appearance of that essence, its expression in symptoms, its coloring, depend on current cultural and institutional factors. As we have discussed, the socially alienated of the Middle Ages were linked to religious modes of disorder and attacked as demons and witches. In an age of rationalism, the same illnesses could be approached in highly intellectual terms, categorized as brain disorders and termed dementia praecox. Psychodynamic psychiatry must be kept in perspective as man's *contemporary* understanding of man. Since it is an evolutionary science, it will reach beyond as well as incorporate preceding approaches to mental illness, and we must assess its relevance in the present while expecting continued and unpredictable shifts in its future development.

THE SCIENCE OF PSYCHODYNAMIC PSYCHIATRY

Our Basic Science

Most clinical sciences of medicine have a basic science which is discrete. For example, vascular physiology provides clinical cardiology with experimental data detailing the impact of alterations in heart rate or peripheral resistance. Psychodynamic psychiatry has no such separate, basic aspect. We provide our own laboratory for the accumulation of data and the development of hypotheses and simultaneously we are basic and clinical in our approach. The ongoing doctor-patient relationship is that laboratory with data gathered from the communications which develop and from the shifts of psychic forces which occur in the patient as well as the doctor. Our clinical science is psychotherapy. In that setting, we are utilizing our theoretical knowledge to promote recovery from psychic illness.

Within our clinical laboratory we have certain research tools. These include observation of behavior, collection of biographic material, consideration of sequential meanings, and exploration of affective expressions. Such instruments are only as valid as the prowess of the physician; for the unfamiliar and inexperienced the tools appear to be a welter of confusing and perhaps mysterious devices, devoid of intent or rational purpose. The novice uses the tools of psychodynamic psychiatry only with awkwardness and lack of comprehension. For example, a grasp of our basic science is necessary to follow a patient who describes hearing voices. There may be changes in source as well as in intonation during hallucinations. The sources, the affective shifts, and the content changes are each items of information. They require a systematic pursuit according to a thought-out procedure of investigation. Questioning, selectively emphasizing, and recasting each have their part in assembling such data.

Our methodology as a basic science varies with a patient's situation and style of relating, with the current setting of the treatment relationship, and of course with the experience, personality, and theoretical orientation of the physician. No simple formula of history taking, or symptom inventory, or stepwise procedure is appropriate. The data must be gathered with the focus on the needs of the patient, needs which are met by the psychotherapist in a way which will establish a relationship within which information is gathered. The nature of the treatment relationship is itself a major portion of the data. In some clinical investigations, one combines chosen known elements with unknown substances in a particular manner in order to discover the nature of the unknown substance. In our "experiments," the psychic unknowns are evaluated in a known clinical setting (the interview situation with the physician) to determine the approximate nature of the patient's psychic functioning.

Having achieved the data collection by means of our clinical methodology, the investigator constructs his hypotheses and tests them through further inquiry, clarifications, and interpretations. Validation is obtained by the gathering of new information which substantiates and elaborates original formulation.

Our Applied Sciences

Psychotherapy is the clinical application of our basic science of psychodynamics. It commences at the first encounter of doctor and patient and cannot be temporally separated from the process of investigation we have discussed. It *can* be conceptually separated since the basic science strives to gather data and formulate, to diagnose, while the applied science concerns itself with influencing forces of the mind. But as early became apparent to Freud,[3] one cannot expose significant mental processes without changing their interaction; the ego defenses which have kept memories hidden are the very resistances and distortions which become altered during investigation. The clinical approach becomes a constant cycle of observation, investigation, formulation, intervention, and alteration followed by further observation—leading to repetition of the cycle.

Both patient and doctor must gain a capacity to focus on their own experiences, their own hypotheses, and learn to become observers of their own reactions and expectations. Both must become persons who circulate their experience internally and exchange their observations in the struggle toward the change of behavioral patterns. Initial changes occur through the corrective ego experience, the therapist supplying ego where weaknesses have been observed. The patient and his physician uncover the feelings which have been intolerable and as the relationship becomes established, the therapist must recognize that the focus of these feelings inevitably will be turned upon him in force. At this point, the patient and therapist learn together to bear the intense feelings thus generated through rigorous attention to the detail of painful life events. A constant empathic awareness of unspoken feelings within the relationship is reviewed to bring them to conscious attention. By helping the patient locate within his own self the affects he is currently experiencing, the therapist allows the patient to acknowledge them for what they are, to bear them in relation to the objects to whom they belong, and to gain perspective on the situation.

REFLECTIONS ON OUR SCIENCE

The science of psychodynamics is young and controversial. Different points of view on the significance of organic, psychosocial, and of inherited factors in the etiology and in the treatment of mental illness divide American psychiatry into numerous apparently antagonistic groupings. Consensus exists on the necessity for persistent study of the entire complex of forces—biological, psychological, or environmental—influencing human behavior. The ongoing synthesis of knowledge which is crucial to the growth of psychiatry can only be weakened if we are isolated from the disparate trends of thought represented in behaviorism, existentialism, or community psychiatry.

There are several allied disciplines which deserve particular mention. Academic psychology has produced a multitude of nonclinical experiments and approaches to problems of behavior which have had limited impact on our practice. Investigation of pigeon responses may seem irrelevant to psychoses, but certainly we have much to learn from the methodology of experimental psychology. Sociology, anthropology, and ethnology have extended the framework of dynamic theory into areas of culture and environment with investigations which seem to confirm many assumptions, to misapply others, and to give reason for re-examination of still others. Physiological study of emotion has advanced concurrently with our understanding of anxiety and sadness. The technical devices which allow the physiologist to differentiate skin resistances or minimal changes in heart rate will certainly become useful to our investigation of egos overwhelmed by intolerable feelings. Neurophysiology, electroencephalography, and psychodynamic psychiatry are combining their special interests in researchers in dream labs. Already new hypotheses about REM states and their importance in the economy of energy raise questions about the clinical management of the sleepless turmoils of our patients. Pharmacological advances have drastically altered the inpatient populations of our hospitals. Medicine and surgery present us with few clarifications and many questions about psychosomatic illness. We must struggle to communicate to colleagues in these fields how anxiety influences physical homeostasis. Neurochemistry and neurophysiology may delineate the biochemistry of the brain more exactly, but Seymour

Kety has indicated the obvious tangential influence of such findings on dynamic psychiatry: "There may be a biochemistry of memory but not of memories."[4]

Research and assessment of therapeutic results have been underdeveloped areas of psychodynamic psychiatry. We are accustomed to attacks from colleagues who have a less than complete grasp of our objectives. Other sciences have ordered their data and refined their hypotheses to make significant strides by drastically reducing variables. We cannot generalize from a single level of investigation of psychic forces. For instance, in studying the improvement of paranoid schizophrenic persons it would be tempting to limit investigation to the disappearance of hallucinations. But the concurrent interpersonal aspects, the appearance of depressive feelings, and the amount of overt hostility toward real people are indeed necessary simultaneous dimensions and cannot be "controlled" in a clinical study. Techniques are required which approach multivariant processes without being simplistic to the extent that answers are prejudiced by the design of questions. One can anticipate that the application of data-processing approaches will produce new hypotheses for investigation. Additional breakthroughs rely not only on refinement of methodology but also on new tools for the collection of information. Open-ended group therapy programs, the use of video and audio recording, and epidemiologic investigations give clues of future tools which may assume importance in our science. In line with Charcot's rule, one must broaden investigative perspective by staring at the data after you get it, ready to go beyond the primary technique by applying others. Thus, the apparent contradictions between several perspectives on various aspects of psychoses may lessen as synthesis permits broader points of view.

LEARNING THE CLINICAL APPROACH

The beginning student of psychodynamic psychiatry requires his own opportunity to research, to hypothesize, and to reformulate our discipline. His treatment of patients becomes his classroom-laboratory for the investigation of psychodynamic principles. Supervision is the complicated pedagogy through which the beginner acquires familiarity with and develops proficiency in the basic as well as the applied sciences.

Supervision begins with the structuring of collected data into significant frameworks. The paucity of information will lead to questions of how to collect data in order to obtain a broader and broader base for diagnostic hypothesis. An *empathic diagnosis* is crucial. It requires a capacity to feel oneself into the patient's dilemma and to appreciate the painful experiences, ideas, and affects avoided in the impaired state of the patient's ego functioning. The beginning resident may attempt treatment before he achieves an empathic diagnosis; he may mistake his own conceptual skills for technical competence. He needs his supervisor as one who can catalyze the learning process, provide necessary guidelines and reference points, and help him validate his researches. By mixing, fusing, and crystallizing observed facts with knowledge, theories, and experiences, the supervisor helps the therapist become available to the patient even as learning commences.

The depth of rapport must be carefully assessed. The supervisor struggles to determine with the resident just what level of relationship, degree of activity, and amount of support is required to enable a patient to face and withstand pain. As he becomes involved with his patient, the resident experiences unaccustomed feelings that require his supervisor's assistance in bearing, formulating, and determining appropriate responses to these affects. Early anxiety, self-devaluation, and taking personally the reactions of his patients present formidable blocks to learning about psychodynamic psychiatry. The skills needed to become a seasoned therapist are slowly developed through errors and disappointments, and most psychiatrists require around 10 years to grow into maturity. Perhaps the greatest contribution from psychoanalysis to the psychotherapy of the psychoses has been through analysis of the infantile components of *therapists'* personalities. By enlarging command of conscious correctives, such an analysis makes it possible that a trained psychotherapist approaches patients with tolerance, mutual affective understanding, and a greater capacity to feel himself into the conflicts of the overwhelmed and regressed person. This enrichment of the skills of therapists will continue to bring psychodynamic theory a little nearer to some exact psychological truth.

Differences in theoretical bias and in therapeutic approach are obvious both among psychiatric teaching centers and between supervisors. The individual resident provides startling evidences of our historical roots as he develops and becomes comfortable in his profession. In spite of the caution of his seniors, the first-year resident often demonstrates a zealous commitment to cure. "If I can only give enough, love enough, interpret enough, then my patient will get well,"—so runs the rationale of these powerful impulses to rescue. It is a humanism which is little tempered by experience, but which may provide the motive force for mastering our demanding science. A resident may be driven to spiritistic and nearly magical approaches by great quantities of his own and his patient's feelings. Impatient with the complexity of the mind, he may grasp at an organic disease, at hypnosis, or at an oversimplified cultural factor to explain the chaos of the schizophrenic person. Or he may catalog and categorize without grasp of the significance of unconscious factors or affective exchanges. Laboring without a frame of reference adequate to bring perspective into his experiences, the beginner turns to external forces to relieve his internal distress. As he develops his capacity for empathy and can use his personality as an instrument to diagnose and respond to a patient's needs, he approaches the current theoretical position of psychodynamics.

There is a parallel between the developing resident in relation to his eventual identity as a psychiatrist and the human embryo in relation to the mature man. The human embryo will pass through outmoded phases of reptile-like and monkey-like shape before assuming human form. The resident will struggle through some of the periods of our science's evolution before he reaches his own personal form of professional competency. Ontogeny recapitulates phylogeny; our humanness includes our evolutionary precursors. The growth of the resident recapitulates the development of our science of psychodynamic psychiatry.

REFERENCES

1. Gittelson, Maxwell: Psychoanalysis and dynamic psychiatry. AMA Arch. Neurol. Psychiat. 66:280–288, 1951.
2. Semrad, Elvin V.: The role of the psychoanalyst in supervising psychotherapy. In: On the Role of the Psychoanalyst in Supervising Psychotherapy. Proceedings of the Fouth Onchiota Conference. June 19–21, 1964.
3. Freud, Sigmund: Introductory Lectures on Psycho-Analysis (1916-1917). Standard Edition, Vols. 15 and 16. London, Hogarth Press, 1963.
4. Kety, Seymour S.: A biologist examines the mind and behavior approach to psychopathology: In: Page, James D. (Ed.): Approaches to Psychopathology. New York, Columbia University Press, 1966, pp. 271–296.

CHAPTER II

A Clinical Formulation of the Psychoses

By Elvin V. Semrad, M.D.

Psychosis-Vulnerability

To grasp the personality factors significant in the decompensation of persons subject to psychosis, we observe the florid psychosis and the recovery process. One can confidently describe a cluster of structural qualities in ego functioning which these persons share and which leave them vulnerable to ego disorganization. Other specifics of personality development and of character type along with the precipitating stresses influence the symptoms of the psychosis and lead to exact classification. In light of reactions to hallucinogens, to concentration camps, and to sensory deprivation we assume that the ego weaknesses which concern us are common in mild degrees and may persist without crippling effect. Vulnerability is a latent quality of a person's ego; the occurrence of an individually significant stress is necessary to produce a manifest psychosis.

In therapy with these people we observe aspects of relationship which reveal ego defects. Their ego-executant pat-

17

terns of behavior betray avoidances of affect and of involvement with others which might demand feeling. *There is in the patient's personality structure extant at any given moment an incapacity to acknowledge, bear, put, and keep in perspective and control by either ordinary or neurotic mechanisms certain distressing affects associated with aloneness, depression and the inevitable and unchangeable sources of life dissatisfactions which can become overwhelming.* To the alert therapist the side-stepping of human involvement is a signal of a need. By providing the necessary support, the therapist permits the patient to bear the intolerable feelings. The patient will gradually reveal the techniques he uses to avoid those affects which have been too much for his unsupported ego.

The sources of this inability to bear certain feelings are discovered in infantile experiences which left a lasting imprint on the developing ego. Anna Freud[1] has discussed "object anxiety," and we find this a part of the pathogenic situations concerning us. The ego-executant structures of the very young child indeed are easily overwhelmed by rage or dread or terror. Spitz[2] has shown how reliant the infant is on a consistent maternal object. Winnicott[3] has detailed the response of the infant to early prolonged separation: protest (an *active* ego response) is supplanted by despair and in pathological situations a child remains detached and distrustful. When a primary relationship failed to provide, the ego endured by shutting itself off, by directing some of its pain against itself, and by blunting its sensitivity to interpersonal disappointments. Evoked and re-evoked as such an ego response must be in the course of life, a fixed and pathological posture developed in our patients. Just as the deserted infant may come to refuse food, so our patients in their particular manner may avoid everyday relationships or aspects of life which might awaken the old unbearable pain.

Ego-conversion[4] is a term we use to denote the process of handling affect in these pathogenic alterations. Unable to rely on immature discharge mechanisms for the expression of internal pain, a crippling—almost paralytic—stifling of reaction to major emotion occurs. Whether it is an internal impulse threatening to overload the ego, or an external danger requiring protective activity, the altered apparatus cannot give its attention, circulate its response, or focus its energy on the reality demands. Flight becomes reflex. The unbearable of the outside induces a change in the self, a changed attitude to perception, emotion, and action. This amounts to a continuing pain of existence which requires defensive organization just to avoid and which saps the ego of energy for constructive living. Such patterns of ego-executant behavior persist and appear at the wrong time, with the wrong person, in the wrong place or in exaggerated form to betray the vulnerability of the person's development. A posture erected to survive psychic pain may persist as a core of avoidance. The limitations in reality integration and in personal flexibility are one day great enough to necessitate psychotic behavior, since old and infantile conversions become inadequate for new and adult life stresses. Progressively, life entails more losses and frustrations, and affects of aloneness become a part of everyday life. But these defective egos remain highly dependent on objects for a continual flow of sustenance, support, and gratification.

Responses of avoidance and avoidance actions are the common denominators of these psychosis-vulnerable egos. The ego is specialized in getting away from what hurts, either retreating from exposure to stimuli or desperately trying to nullify the impact of the painful by activity. For these egos, psychoses are the extreme, grotesque, and pathetic disasters revealing flaws in development which had often remained inapparent. A continuum of clinical illness from schizophrenia to neurotic reaction is observed and depends on the effectiveness of ego-executant patterns, the nature of the crystallizations in avoidance behavior, and the particular variety of stressful event. Recovery from a schizophrentic illness will inevitably proceed through some affective stages resembling the depressive psychoses, and our grouping of psychoses into "schizophrenia" and "depressive psychosis" is for purposes of exposition while we presume an intertwining of problems in their treatment.

SCHIZOPHRENIA

The Schizophrenia-
Vulnerable Person

In their avoidance, the personalities of these people have relied on a *narcissistic triad of ego defenses:* denial, projection, and distortion. *Denial* is a refusal to perceive. By not turning one's mind to the undesirable stimulus, the individual has prevented any internal turmoil from occurring. In neuronal terms, the afferent impulse never ascends to the central body. We distinguish this primitive defense from repression where the perception *is* received in the ego but is retained out of consciousness and sidetracked for future reference and impact. Denial has usefulness in protecting the self from external danger: it produces severe handicaps when internal affect is handled as if it likewise was an external danger. Therefore, capacity to delay response, to circulate painful experiences, and to dissipate tension within the body are developed to a limited extent only. Without such precursors, repression cannot become the cornerstone of social and intellectual development in latency years. Instead, these egos are constricted in their perceptions. The characteristic "schizoid" pattern of shunning relationships or abruptly halting them is one result of these primitive means of controlling danger. In adolescent years an extreme concentration on science or narrowness of solitary hobbies (be they stamps or cars) may reveal the deep-seated reliance on patterns which wall off the individual.

Projection is closely linked with denial, the ego protecting itself against danger by laying responsibility for unacceptable drives and faults at the door of external agents. The projections defend against guilty anxiety, guilt about "base" inclinations which cannot be acknowledged as one's own, as well as against excitement such as may be experienced when one is close to others. The aggressive responses of paranoid persons are commonly a warding off of the desires for intimacy.

Distortion patterns are attempts at consolation for affection not received. Day-dreaming, self-flattering delusions, and ready resort to fantasy formation are reconstructions of reality to satisfy wishes which are unattainable since the grappling with real relationships is so fraught with unbearable feeling. The energy demanded by such reverie is lost to the commerce of getting along with people.

Identification with the aggressor is a major source of vulnerability to schizophrenia. Heavy reliance on this pattern prevents the development of adequate neutralization and of ego-ideal identifications. Relationships of early childhood with their enormous burdens of feeling were resolved by ingestion without digestion. Immaturity did demand harmony to assure survival and the cost of love from parents was blind acceptance of their ways. The "unquestioning" aspect of this introjection masks ambivalence and is effective to contain rage only so long as the interdependent deception persists. It often requires the actual presence of the primary object or her substitute. The symbiosis is deep and rewarding to parent as well as to child, but the losses of time or the realities of growth bring a shattering of the balance to aggressive impulses and annihilation of the mother emerges as a wish. A continuing supply of sustenance, support, and gratification from outside does offset the rage, but should it cease, the vulnerable person loses part of his ego and his defective personality cannot neutralize an overwhelming negative reaction.

The formation of stable ego-ideals has been thwarted by the constant ambivalence of relationships. The self may be sacrificed in each new transaction by *ego repression*. To make sure that his objects love him, and thus to maintain a sense of feeling loved, he imitates the other in awkward and unstudied ways. This primitive kind of identification defers the maturing of his personality since ideals remain external to himself and do not represent his own choices.

Either deprivation or overindulgence—the extremes of parent-infant loving—can foster this pathological development. In the adult who is *deprived* in his early years, we find patterns of ambivalence bursting forth when losses are experienced. Self-esteem is low, helplessness becomes great, and he fails to feel in charge of himself or to trust himself as master of his destiny. He finds himself in a paralyzing uncertainty as to the affection and respect of others; he finds himself inhibited in speaking out only to periodically demand in clumsy and ungracious ways. Having avoided the pain of interpersonal relationships by aggressive identifications, he now finds himself in a position of more loss, more threat, more hate, and more projected hate. The world of people becomes even more dangerous once he worries that others will discover him loathesome and poisonous.

Reliance on identification with the aggressor is also strong in the *overindulged*. In early years these schizophrenia-vulnerable persons experienced frustration of their strivings to autonomy and were deprived of a realistic milieu such as is essential if a child is to develop appropriate responsiveness to other's feelings. Particularly offensive assertions, demandingness, grasping, and megalomanic expectations of others mask the ego's limitations in mutual understanding and useful self-assertion which might communicate with rather than grab on to others. Like the deprived group, their defective powers of neutralization cannot withstand the affect accompanying failures of existence and they hate, project their hate, and become estranged.

Precipitation of the
Schizophrenic Psychosis

Stresses, losses, crucial life events, and the pain of any of these overwhelm our vulnerable persons leaving them inundated by unbearable affect. The nature of the stress may seem trivial, but the personal early avoidances and affective experiences make it a subjective holocaust. The narcissistic defenses (denial, projection, and distortion) become more evident and although not effective in dealing with the realities, they strive to maintain a massive avoidance of the unbearable affect.

Ego decompensation,[5] regression, and clinical psychosis occur in periods of *intensification of affect*.[6] Unpleasure increases and re-evokes the impossible pain of early relationship. The burden is intensified by the liberation of previously unbearable affects. Once integration with reality crumbles and our patient enters a disorganized and exhausting state of psychophysiological pain which he never could bear, other solutions are demanded. All that is open to the vulnerable ego at this point is suicide, murder, or psychosis. Suicide or murder are the extreme expression of affect (principally rage) translated into action; psychosis is the partially rationalized containment of the affect, the sacrifice of reality to preserve life.

Initially the unpleasure may be so intense that the ego is overwhelmed, left immobile, and without enough organization to repress or contain in any sense. In this state, the ego cannot store the traumatic event in its memory. It cannot effect modification of the real world for its advantage. It cannot control its pain or stem overwhelming feeling. It cannot find comfort by manipulating another person. It can only mobilize every resource to avoid unpleasure through flight and through action. It can only repeat its crystallized postures learned under similar stress by the young child's ego.

The clinical manifestations of these psychotic ego patterns are classified into descriptive groups according to the preponderant narcissistic defense observed. The catatonic person in his "not minding" remains in the stunned state as if without capacity for action. The paranoid person projects: since he cannot bear his pain he bids that others share his responsibility. The acutely deluded person refuses perspective on the intensified affect, flees into make-believe, and wishes that the unbearable were something it is not. The person in turmoil is between wanting to stay and wanting to flee: his inability to neutralize the ambivalence of relationship is evident in the constant debate between the mature and the overwhelmed portions of his ego.

Before schizophrenia becomes chronic schizophrenia, a way of life, the ego fights to regain reality in preference to pursuing the self-consoling activity of psychotic transformation. In his nightmarish struggle to bolster his toehold in actual life events, the acute patient tends to a restitutive posture even in his language, symbols, and symptoms. Since he is predominantly ambivalent, he simultaneously discloses and denies his ideas and feelings. He cries for help and abuses the outstretched hand. Issues of pain and of assistance in surmounting pain are charged with dread and fear of rejection; therefore, the need to disguise and to negate any plea for help. The healthy capacity to feel what there is to be felt, to think what there is to be thought, and to circulate these through one's total experience is replaced by cautious, erratic phrases and private language which make some of these communications dubiously comprehensible and others incomprehensible. Bizarre irrelevancies or cryptic neologisms often prove to be verbal expressions of intolerable body sensations. This communication through unclear words involves the whole mechanism of language in the service of hiding while at the same time saying what the patient wants to say.[7]

The chronic schizophrenic person finds himself at an impasse in the matter of communication. He does not want to know. He does not want to feel. He does not want to think about the unbearable affect-laden issues. And he relentlessly denies the potential of others to help. The more chronic the clinical condition, the more solidified the stance, and the more the communications have become negative and unintelligible.

PSYCHOTIC DEPRESSION

Vulnerability to Psychotic Depression

The obsessional characteristics of the psychotically depressed person may be strongly colored with narcissism, but when properly supported as in treatment the patient will acknowledge his reality.[8] Such interaction, a giving up of primitive avoidance, contrasts with the entrenched denial of the more schizoid character. The psychotically depressed person has endured it by making other people share his pain and has convinced them that circumstances were against him. The person vulnerable to schizophrenia, however, projects without caution as to what others will find acceptable reasons for projection. In a psychotic depression, reality is perceived without gross and unequivocal distortion: an omnipotent misconstruction occurs particularly in object relationships to deny dependence while achieving sustenance. Contempt and depreciation of important family members or of a therapist betray this need for tyrannical control.

These patients do have ego structures heavily weighted with the triad of narcissistic defenses, particularly distortion, yet significantly less so than is seen in persons vulnerable to schizophrenia. By virtue of maneuvers which manipulate others to their support, they have developed during their total experience of relationships a greater integration of personality. We term the pertinent ego patterns of activity an *affective triad of ego defenses:* compulsive-obsessive pattern, hypochondriacal pattern, and neurasthenic pattern. All are seen in psychotic depressions as well as in the recovering schizophrenic, and their consideration cannot be restricted to affective illnesses.

In the overuse of compulsive actions and mechanisms,[9] our patients are in particular trying to contain the conscious distress of guilty anxiety, a reverberation of the relatively unconscious resentments against objects needed for security. The degree of compulsion in acts of goodness, appeasement, or perfectionistic rituals roughly approximates the degree of guilt or anxiety produced by unacknowledged aggressive wishes. But such solutions are inadequate to bind temptations to attack loved ones and our patients regress to make-believe. A pretense of problem-solving may accompany their overactivity, which in fact only allays tension. For all their goodness, humility, and appeasement, these people are far from convincing: they give a great deal of trouble, perpetually take offense, and behave as if treated with great injustice.

The hypochondriacal patterns solicit sympathy, affection, and emotional support through mutual concern over physical function.[9] Fearful that their personal merits will not hold the love of an object, they develop body weaknesses which demand investment of libido from outside. The mutual activity of nursing and being sick assures and excuses the persistence of the dependent relationship. In the childhoods of these persons, we find periods of convalesence from significant illnesses where this pattern was cultivated, making this an "actual" neurosis during its crystallization. A fertile source for bodily complaints lies also in the physiological expressions of anxiety such as gas pains, pulse irregularity, skin flushing, or hyperventilation. The ego of the person vulnerable to psychotic depression comes to rely on this pattern in its management of the fine line between feeling itself compensated rather than overwhelmed, that fine line between a personality operating at a belabored optimum as compared to one beginning to decompensate and experience intolerable affects.

We also see in the affective triad of defensive organization neurasthenic patterns of behavior.[10] The inception of this pattern is in that period of early childhood when acceptance by mother becomes linked with her expectation of performance. Bowel training is the most apparent negotiation of this issue, and the withholding features of neurasthenia reflect the refusal to grant the demand to use the pot. In anticipation of frustration or failure in adult encounters, these people magnify difficulties and profess fatigue, ineptitude, or misunderstanding to protect their avoidance.

The primarily neurotic patterns—the *neurotic triad*—of dissociation, organ conversion, and anxiety manifestations are present in these patients as attempts to restore repression in the service of avoiding unbearable feeling. As with those vulnerable to schizophrenia, the relative unsuccess of such more mature patterns may be seen in the overwhelmed ego of the psychotically depressed person where repression vital for the neurotic defenses cannot contain affects as they occur. In the less vulnerable person, as well as in our vulnerable patients encountering a personally less important loss, we find the reactions classified as neurotic depression where the defense of repression continues to be effective.

Precipitation of Psychotic Depression

The vulnerable person is deprived of essential support when he loses a crucial object or when a major need for an object is frustrated. He suffers an extraordinary fall in self esteem: a loss of ego has occurred. The painful affect of separation, the sadness and aloneness for so long staved off by manipulations, now floods the ego. Perhaps as a result of oral incorporation of the beloved, aggressive feelings for the object are turned against the patient's self as identified with the object and give us the self-accusations, the expiations, the head-beating so common in these psychotic persons. Libidinal energy is absorbed in the work of mourning,[11] leaving little for zest, for outward-oriented action, or for personal goals. His ego is in a state of real or imagined helplessness facing overwhelming odds, for the painful discovery of not being loved or not being independent has regressively evoked the primary feeling of helplessness in the gratification of narcissistic needs. The revolt against loss initially apparent in his behavior has developed into a mental constellation beyond mere contrition and has overwhelmed reality in its full forcefulness.

Mania

The person vulnerable to manic-depressive episodes differs most from one vulnerable to psychotic depression in the character of his dependence on infantile love objects. The manic requires a supporting object, rather than a sustaining object, and he evidences more capacity for unaided survival and utilization of ego strengths. The psychotically depressed person will feel at times—perhaps permanently—that he cannot live without his object: the loss of the relationship is the end of the world. The manic-depressive offsets his feelings of unworthiness by a constant supply of love and of moral support from his object, and while the object lasts he functions with enthusiasm and high efficiency. When he loses that object, his compulsive activity patterns prevent a flooding of the ego with despair. The overactivity, overtalkativeness, and flight of ideas of mania is a compulsive action oriented to the avoidance of introspection, to the denial of inner painful reality, and to the maintenance of attention on external reality. This pattern relieves tension but does not solve problems. Since all effort is bent on not becoming aware of his own feelings, he cannot empathize with others and becomes emotionally isolated and retaliatively anxious. If the behavior becomes more psychotic, it is hard to distinguish from "catatonic excitement," and it is only in the manic's more purposeful flight into action to relieve inner despair that we may differentiate him from the more schizophrenic person.[12]

The characteristic avoidances or action patterns are rarely so straightforward or present in pure culture. A psychotherapist must be constantly shifting from a conceptual framework of ego defenses and data collected to support a given construct in terms of avoidance to an empathic sensitivity to needs for therapeutic intervention. The science of psychodynamics gives the physician a rational basis upon which to make these shifts.

REFERENCES

1. Freud, Anna: The Ego and the Mechanisms of Defence. New York, International Universities Press, 1946.
2. Spitz, René: The First Year of Life. New York, International Universities Press, 1965.
3. Winnicott, D. W.: Transitional objects and transitional phenomena. Int. J. Psychoanal. 34:89-97, 1953.
4. Mann, James, and Semrad, Elvin V.: Conversion as process and conversion as symptom in psychosis. In: Deutsch, Felix (Ed.): On the Mysterious Leap from the Mind to the Body. New York, International Universities Press, 1959, pp. 131-154.
5. Semrad, Elvin V., and Zaslow, Stephen L.: Assisting psychotic patients to recompensate. Ment. Hosp. 15:361-366, 1964.
6. Freud, Sigmund: The Neuro-Psychoses of Defence (1894). Standard Edition, Vol. 3. London, Hogarth Press, 1962, pp. 41-61.
7. Arsenian, John, and Semrad, Elvin V.: Schizophrenia and language. Psychiat. Quart. 40:449-458, 1966.
8. Semrad, Elvin V.: Some observations about psychotic depression. Paper read at Institute of Living, Hartford, Connecticut, April 18, 1961, and at Albert Einstein College of Medicine, Bronx Municipal Hospital Center Departmental Conference-University Professors Series, New York, May 25, 1961. In process of publication.
9. Bibring, Edward: The mechanism of depression. In: Greenacre, Phyllis (Ed.): Affective Disorders. New York, International Universities Press, 1953, pp. 13-48.
10. Semrad, Elvin V.: Discussion of Part I—Problems in discharge planning for patients in hospitals. In: Greenblatt, Milton, Levinson, Daniel J., and Klerman, Gerald L. (Eds.): Mental Patients in Transition. Springfield, Ill., Charles C Thomas, 1961, pp. 46-48.
11. Freud, Sigmund: Mourning and Melancholia (1917). Standard Edition, Vol. 14. London, Hogarth Press, 1957, pp. 237-260.
12. Mack, John E., and Semrad, Elvin V.: Classical psychoanalysis. In: Freedman, Alfred M. and Kaplan, Harold I. (Eds.): Comprehensive Textbook of Psychiatry. Baltimore, Williams & Wilkins, 1967, pp. 269-319.

CHAPTER III

Comments on Psychotherapy of the Psychoses

By Elvin V. Semrad, M.D.

Any application of psychotherapeutic maneuvers of suggestion, abreaction, manipulation, clarification, and interpretation[1] depends on a careful assessment of ego factors such as those discussed in the preceding chapter. Usually one expects a consensus between patient and therapist of the need for treatment with each able to cooperate, understand, and pursue a common endeavor. But if by dint of his psychosis, a patient is mute or abusive, terrified or suspicious, he may not be verbally communicative to his physician. Many gifted therapists have been prevented from treating psychotic persons by awkwardness in approaching these initial phases of treatment.

The therapist's first concern must be to develop and maintain a relationship which will meet the patient's fundamental needs of sustenance, support, and gratification, the disruption of which has led to a psychotic regression. To do this, the therapist explores his patient's wants and thus discovers ways in which intervention will be accepted. This *empathic diagnosis* is the process of feeling oneself into the patient's dilemma to discover the painful experiences, ideas, and affects avoided by the fragmented ego and often appearing as an avoidance of help from a therapist.

The very signals observed often confound individuals. In normal or neurotic individual one notices anxiety in response to frustration and psychic pain, anxiety which is adaptively expressed in and allayed by neurotic defense. Psychotic patients deny such signal anxiety and the corresponding communication is often a flight from people or a bizarre seeking of objects for relief. Increases of unpleasure in vulnerable persons are handled by specialized outside activity to disengage or to involve others rather than by internal psychic or somatic readjustments as seen in neurotic persons. The therapist observes in hospitalized patients a body response of helplessness where the patient's unpleasure has mounted in the absence of required relationship. As unpleasure increases further and the ego is overwhelmed, the patient's signal has been a body response of disintegration, dread, terror, fear, or panic. An empathic diagnosis searches to determine if the patient is inviting the therapist forward or is doing everything in his power to maintain the status quo—the homeostasis or constancy required to survive—and thus is terrified by the proximity of a new object. The avoidance activity may indeed be the most desperate of cries for help.

Techniques, Resistances, and Transference

Interpretation with these patients is utilized very early in therapy in the service of making the relationship. A bit of data offers a clue to the chain of events which led to psychosis, and the therapist communicates his construction of that process to promote reintegration and to support the pain of living and the stresses of existence. Enabling the patient to discover significances in early experiences leads to a gradual restoration of the continuum of past, present, and future. The psychosis is an emergency pattern of behavior in the face of overwhelming affect, a declaration of ego ineptitude. In contrast, the therapist's interpretations demonstrate his capacity to handle such feelings. The wild impulses of the patient become conceptualized in the words of the physician, and thus an opportunity is presented for the patient to consider, to defer, to examine alternatives, and *to not act*. The process of verbal interventions by the therapist will eventually enable the patient to think on his own.

> A college student who was hospitalized for wildly destructive behavior became solitary and aloof in the hospital. He was noted to mumble lying on his bed. "You won't. You hate me. You forced me to." Knowing that this man's roommate had recently been drafted, and that his father had been overseas in the army from the time the patient was 7 until he was 11, the therapist commented that the patient felt lonely and mad and that it would be hard for him to expose his feelings. The therapist wondered what he talked of in his conversations, and the nature of his hallucinations gradually unfolded. After a few weeks he revealed that he hated the roommate for deserting him, and he began to discuss his fears of closeness which could be traced back to his father and the disruption of that relationship.

The patient comes to utilize experiences with his therapist. Later he begins to find himself separately by observation of the doctor's person and by searching for contrasts in signals and feelings. In a sense, the psychosis is the patient's cry of pain demanding direct gratification of needs for survival. In therapy these needs may be met with direct sustenance of ego activities through personal participation.

Confrontation is used to call attention to behavior which is not appropriate or is not ego-syntonic, behavior which constitutes a breach in an otherwise reasonable facade. So often the resistance is an alibi, an attempt to rationalize the unacceptable into plausibility. The need to deny such contradictions and to avoid affects of close contact militates against the occurrence of a classical transference neurosis. In fact, a common form of *countertransference* problem is a therapist excessive in his zeal to pin down reality by ordering his patient to be consistent and honest. The patient's behavior will demonstrate resistances and thus betray what he verbally avoids. The interruptions in narrating a life story, the breaking of an appointment, the request for a cigarette, the visits to other doctors may each reveal an unsuspected but important affect which is not otherwise acknowledged in treatment. The therapist listens to what is not said, searches actual experience for relevances, and states his perceptions to the patient in order to clarify what has been avoided. In a hospital setting, material for mutual discussion must include pertinent information about behavior as gathered from all sources especially during the early months of treatment.

Transference presents a definite infantile aspect which requires special consideration. The search for a "good enough mother," as Winnicott has put it,[2] is met by demonstrations that the therapist cares, protects, and sustains, communicated in whatever manner is personally suitable to therapist and patient. Sometimes a gift such as an extra appointment or even an apple, sometimes a definite prohibition of an ill-fated or premature action may be needed to maintain the collaboration toward the development of an integrated ego. A "delusional transference" reveals the dissatisfaction the patient is experiencing. It must be approached as an index of contact disquietude, as an indicator that somatic conversion processes are inadequate and the vulnerable ego has resorted to narcissistic defenses. Interpretation of these transference reactions must be oriented to the current capacity of the vulnerable ego to encounter reality for what it is as opposed to what the needs of the patient would make it.

Countertransference is an intricate problem, and subsequent chapters will consider several aspects of it. A therapist
and a patient are each struggling with the same problem, the
patient's shattered experience, and each has the opportunity
to examine his way of dealing with related areas of anxiety
and conflict. The blind spots of the therapist will vitiate his
effectiveness in either understanding or in communicating just
how it was that his patient could not bear or tolerate or in-
tegrate his misfortunes and responsibilities. When we emphasize
that the empathic therapist must experience with his patient,
we are insisting on the relevance of intuition and feeling to
interpretation. There is always the danger that the therapist
too will act out rather than bear heavy loads of feeling. The
therapist must respect the limits of therapeutic action; that is
to say he must not indulge in emotional seduction or covert
punishment. But the extreme stance of the therapist massively
controlling his feelings and denying his own conflicts prevents
mutuality. The more he compulsively analyzes, the more the
beginner may separate himself from his patient as a human
being. The more he participates with understanding of his
own responsiveness, the more possibility for creative interplay
and useful experiencing comes into the treatment situation.
Emotional interchange indeed becomes an affective coming
together in which the two participants realign their meanings
for each other and see life anew.

> A middle-aged woman was stony and mute, with verbaliza-
> tion centering on body pains and fears of disintegration.
> Her somewhat younger therapist was unsuccessful in estab-
> lishing a relationship when he focused on her husband who
> had died 10 years previously. When he finally suggested to
> this woman that her loneliness had become intolerable after
> her daughter had married and left the patient by herself in
> an "empty nest," the tears came to her eyes and therapeutic
> communication commenced.

NARCISSISTIC DEFENSES IN TREATMENT

The denial patterns appear as "not minding" and require caring and demonstration that the patient in fact matters to the therapist. The personal inclinations and experiences of the therapist determine his approach in proving that he does care.

> A patient had been expelled from law school and could not acknowledge his pain at failure in the real life pursuit of a goal of great fantasy significance. Unable to consider his hurt in any realistic way, he remained in a state of shock. Catatonic, he forced others to care for him in his terror and immobility. His therapist made regular appointments, visited him on the ward, and demonstrated a willingness to sit and wait until the patient felt ready to communicate.

The projection patterns which appear clinically as blaming require the therapist to share the burden of responsibility. The doctor's awareness of, capacity to bear, and to keep in perspective painful ideas and affects do for the patient the seemingly impossible. Literally, the therapist picks up the patient's pain to become a part of the reintegrating pattern of defenses.

> This man's terror gave way to blaming. He was superior to his teachers, the school was antiquated, the courses poorly conceived. One could use the modicum of truth in all this to sustain him by inquiring how it was that he could not fit, and how this had enabled him to bring failure to pass through his own resources. The therapist emphasized for the patient how much he had resented the school. It seemed that no matter how he tried, he could not attain the goals of his fantasy, just as he could not replace his dead father at his mother's side. These fantasies had been bolstered from flimsy wishes into expectations following his father's funeral when his father's best friend had urged the patient to "look after your mother."

Distortion patterns cue the therapist to what is unacceptable about life as it is. He must sensitively weigh the unfulfilled narcissistic expressions and the unbearable pain of life to find avenues for bringing the patient's hurt back to immediacy.

> This man had megalomanic beliefs and hallucinatory experiences which demanded that he act to protect others from danger. Careful pursuit of the suffering over his academic failure enabled the patient to face his future and start from scratch, giving up presumptions of genius. Gradually more aware of his grief, he abandoned his regression and entered a depressive phase.

RECAPITULATION AND REWORKING CHILDHOOD DEVELOPMENT IN TREATMENT

Growth of children proceeds through a succession of relationships oriented to the satisfying of needs. We can roughly distinguish the oral (narcissistic), anal (manipulative), oedipal (genital), and latency (civilized), components of relationships. Each interaction is an attempt to reduce present tension resulting from either inner pain or outer hurt. Our patients are concerned not just with managing quantities of tension; they reflect the rhythm of changes in pleasure and unpleasure and the antecedent problems of managing tension in childhood. As they recover, their relationships parallel those of the child. At any period in life, *sustaining* relationships are needed to survive; *supportive* ones permit individuals to use their strengths to consummate wishes; and *gratifying* relationships emphasize the pleasure of interaction with other persons as individuals.

During the narcissistic period, the infant requires food and shelter from his parents to reduce tension to tolerable levels; the hungry baby screams until mother brings his bottle. With his stomach at rest, he relaxes. In a parallel way, the recovering psychotic person integrates around a sustaining therapist, obtains a period of organ relaxation, visceral harmony, and assured survival.

A 15-year-old girl refused all food, lay about in bed, and cursed her mother. Failing to coax her to the dining room, a night nurse began feeding her baby food by spooning it into her mouth. When her resident therapist learned of this, he too tried spoon feeding. Her manner changed from stubborn negativism and silence to willingness to be fed as a small child. After a week, she followed her physician around the ward, wanting to add more time to her daily half hour with him.

The next developmental task faced by the child is to discover means of manipulating adults to *maintain* the sustaining and supporting relationships. No longer at the complete mercy of grownups, the child can fulfill needs by getting adults to act as he may wish. He pouts until candy is given; he dutifully uses the toilet because mother will kiss him after each bowel movement. Persons in psychotic depressions and recovering from schizophrenic episodes show a parallel reliance on reaction formation in combination with vigorous efforts to control.

A 40-year-old housewife had been reclusive for 3 months. She refused food, lost 30 pounds, muttered and cursed from her bed, and was finally forced to the hospital when her husband felt helpless to cope with his job as well as her and her housework. Their oldest daughter was about to go away to college, and it was she who had cooked the meals and made the beds during the spring of her senior year at high school.

To her therapist, the patient presented a mask of compliance. She was meticulous, although drab, and had a sheaf of notes for each interview. From these she detailed how she had worked and toiled for her husband, helping him with his business, and how she had given parties to encourage her daughter to see more of her classmates. She urged her goodness on to the doctor, but when he wondered about her feeling deserted by her busy family, she ignored him and elaborated her household routine. She needed to make therapy something she could govern. Recognizing the contradictions between her obstinate image of worthiness and her bitter compliance to psychotherapy, the doctor complimented her abilities as a cook and mother. He knowingly let himself become a replacement for the unappreciative daughter who was carrying through on her plan to leave for college. As this woman began to talk of her daughter's lateness, of her curtness about the clothes that mother ironed for her, the therapist carefully avoided judgments about the girl. Instead he explained the hidden craving mother had for her daughter's approval, striving to put the mother's fury at the girl's inevitable independence into perspective as one among many feelings. In a desperate attempt at explanation, the patient spoke of how a teacher had spent hours with the girl, persuading her to go to college in a far off place, and that had it not been for this other woman, her daughter would have been content to go to a local university. The therapist refused to be duped by such a simplistic approach, and he struggled to introduce a balanced view of adolescence, of separation, and of this woman's self-sacrifice as it had developed to maintain herself in her daughter's affection. A frantic effort to squelch the depressive feeling in herself by assurance of love from her therapist followed. "Was she not an excellent mother? Hadn't she done right by her family?" The patient desperately required his approval of her and during a brief lapse in treatment she refused to leave her bed, until the nurses told her she had to get up for meals.

The successful outcome of this period of therapy requires that the love for the internal object be unearthed and tolerated along with the rage experienced when the patient lost that required relationship. The therapist offers respect for effective living and managing feelings and this permits the patient to use his love as the basis for new integration. The energy once invested in the therapist becomes available for current everyday relationships in the course of decathecting and recathecting significant aspects of involvement with past and present persons.

In the oedipal period, the ego of the child should come to terms with the total family, now investing libido beyond survival needs and in relationships demanding recognition of primary objects as persons in their own right. The recovery profiles of patients entering a similar time in therapy greatly depend on pre-morbid strengths and effectiveness. We will often hear discussion or speculation about a therapist's wife or husband, and it is significant to pinpoint the emergence of concern for triangular situations. A neurasthenic phase of being "too tired to go to work" is common, and the therapist must communicate respect for the patient regardless of his performance while underscoring reality considerations.

> A 22-year-old man returned from service in the Navy to find his widowed father remarried to a woman who crabbed at him and indicated that he could expect only a short welcome in her house. He became depressed, panicky, and had homosexual preoccupations. When he became violent, throwing a beer can at his father, he was referred for hospitalization. After several weeks in the hospital he seemed cooperative, accepting, and pleasant. In treatment he discussed his life on the ward, weekends at home, and what it had been like on board ship, but it was always the therapist who mentioned the possibility of his hunting for work. Pressure from vocational counselors sent him to interviews, but he returned to the hospital to lie in bed and complain of exhaustion, pains in his thighs, and constipation. The pattern repeated itself over the next several weeks. Recognizing that his "vegetable state" must be endured—rather than rushed to a conclusion the patient felt unprepared for—the therapist bore with him for many tedious hours of symptom recitation until one day the patient brought in the Sunday want-ads.

Neurotic patterns of anxiety states, organ neuroses, or dissociation may appear during restitution. Their use in the avoidance of affect must always be noted.

Finally, the child learned to invest libido in capacities and activities which guaranteed the presence of substitutive objects. Parents and family moved into the background as new persons at school and at play permitted rewarding interdependent human adaptation by providing the sustenance, support, and gratification. But the human ego never gives up anything; it only adds to its historical positions by mastery of additional interpersonal arrangements for happiness. Inevitably, situations of dependency among people become a market place with a retailing of needs and of gratifications. Where the average child was learning games and trying out friendships during his latency years, many of those persons who later became psychotic had been forced to struggle with issues of survival. The psychosis-vulnerable ego had had little use for experimentation on the playground; in fact ego patterns of avoidance were necessary to control overwhelming feeling. As a patient reintegrates, the therapist acts as a resource and at times as a counselor concerning everyday life. He must be ready to help his patient negotiate outside arrangements. He may discuss job opportunities as they might provide social outlets, encourage membership in church clubs, or point out common tact and courtesy in friendship. A common transition is the grouping together of discharged patients, entertaining, rooming together, dating, and in many ways supporting one another as they leave the security of the hospital behind. This demonstrates a taking of the family into the world at large. But the permanence of the therapist's relationship is often openly sought in denial of the inevitability of termination. A psychotherapist must catalyze his patient to develop friendships beyond treatment, he must point out future possibilities for need satisfactions after therapy, he must communicate his own role as an expert whose provision of gratification is temporary until the ego of the once psychotic person can develop resources elsewhere.

TERMINATION

In the optimal psychotherapy of the psychotic person, treatment proceeds from restitution of ego function (sustained by the therapist) through resumption of ordinary life (supported by the therapist), and finally to analysis of the vulnerable ego. Termination occurs only after several years of gratifying relationship, and we would emphasize that a residency program in moßt hospital settings offer few opportunities to see the later stages of this process or to set dates for termination based on the patient's needs. We see the ultimate separation of therapist and patient as being a matter of concern early in treatment, sometimes not to be verbalized but to be kept in awareness as it may touch on the development of the relationship. Waelder[3] and Nunberg[4] stress love as an ingredient in the optimum synthetic functioning of any given ego—and restitution in treatment requires just such "ego glue." The libidinal intensification evoked by consistent interaction carries its risk of decompensation as well. A patient must test, retest, provoke, and antagonize throughout many phases of therapy in order to discover the nature of this unaccustomed love. He needs the actual experience of the safety of being able to love and to feel loved without violation or punishment. In this process, and overwhelmed by antagonistic impulses and affects, we observe *transference psychoses*—a return to ego fragmentation. Their common occurrence around vacations and the abundance of unresolved feelings we find in connection with them, strengthen our postulation of sustenance as the essential contribution of the therapist to the first phase of treatment.

> A single woman in her thirties became paranoid and depressed when a potentially gratifying relationship with a married superior at her office reached a dead end. After a year's hospitalization and a further year of therapy, her physician announced a vacation. She wondered out loud if she might go along. After his departure she heard that her therapist had just been married. She became overtly psychotic and worried that the FBI wanted her for questioning. She was in a rage at her therapist for she had expected he would one day marry her. Many months of listening to her furor on finding that he could not be available "til death us do part" ensued. The support given to her, the bearing with her grief, permitted her stabilization and the progression of therapy toward consideration of how she had come to invest herself in such one-sided expectations in several relationships.

Eventual termination will be successful where therapy has permitted *reverie* to occur. This is a process in which the wholesale love of primary objects has been retracted to give the patient an opportunity to invest in current positive objects in a bit-by-bit retail fashion. Reverie processes replace all or none worshipful dependencies by the strengthening of real positive relationships. They amount to musing and reliving the primary relationships through current feelings and persons. In the resolution of oedipal conflicts and in the recrudescences in adolescence and marriage, our patients have emphasized negative aspects of relationship to protect themselves from the longing, from the needing, from the eternal temptations of love for the primary object and its repetition.

The success or failure of termination will be seen in the patient's capacity to find actual substitutes for the love given and received in the course of therapy. If libido has been effectively freed from some of the restrictions and contradictions we describe, it will be available for reinvestment in such activities and objects. Appropriate neutralizations will be made to stabilize these new relationships. As treatment ends, grief and separation must be accomplished with all the pain and fear acknowledged. For his part, the therapist communicates his awareness that the crucial techniques of acknowledging, bearing, and putting perspective upon affect which the therapist once supplied to the psychotic person are by now incorporated in the ego of the recovered individual.

It is the challenge of working with these people and watching their growth as they abandon primitive patterns of avoidance in favor of realistic perspective that we pass on to those whom we teach. The treatment and conceptualization of each patient becomes a casebook in itself, but experience demonstrates the common thread of ego conversions, avoidances, and warped patterns of relationship which produce the vicissitudes as well as the opportunities for growth in psychotherapy.

REFERENCES

1. Bibring E. R.: Psychoanalysis and the dynamic psychotherapies. J. Amer. Psychoanal. Assn. 2:745–770, 1954.
2. Winnicott, D. W.: Metapsychological and clinical aspects of regression within the psycho-analytical set-up. Int. J. Psychoanal. 36:16–26, 1955.
3. Waelder, R. The principle of multiple function, Psychoanal. Quart. 5:45, 1936.
4. Nunberg, H. Die Synchetische Funcktion Des Tch. Int. Atsur. Psych. Analytic. 6:25, 1920.

CHAPTER IV

Identity Development in the Beginning Psychiatrist

By David Van Buskirk, M.D.

Those who practice therapy along psychodynamic lines are occasionally called upon to describe their work to nonpsychiatrists. The ready answers include "helping people to grow," "providing a sympathetic ear," or "investigating conflict," with about as many variations as there are psychiatrists. The new resident arrives at our hospital with many such oversimplified conceptions on his mind and with an inclination to tackle the problems in his own way. His recent successful achievement in a complex educational system granted him an M.D. But in many ways that educational process always provided clearcut goals: to be a physician is to have the qualifications to diagnose disease and prescribe medicine, or to be a surgeon is to know medicine and be technically competent to intervene with scalpel and sutures. To become these, one moves through a period of basic, laboratory science on to clinical sciences where a junior physician has junior responsibilities.

As demonstrated in its historical vicissitudes, the specialty of psychiatry possesses no clearcut boundaries and offers no ophthalmoscope or tuning fork to signal accomplishment. To become a psychiatrist is to reach toward a remote identity which will take shape only over years of professional work. The beginner often denies this: he may have to if he is to retain his self-esteem among unfamiliar persons and challenges. A crucial function of the initial supervisor is to assist the new psychiatrist by presenting him with a mature professional image of the psychodynamic psychiatrist. The beginner has before him the supervisor's style and skill as a model to consider. The working through, the growth, the mastering of these challenges occur in a complicated social setting which also influences the outcome of the residents' struggle for identity.

The Hospital Setting

The Massachusetts Mental Health Center—the "Psycho" as it is colloquially and fondly termed from its original name, the Boston Psychopathic Hospital—is an acute treatment center for mentally ill patients located on the edge of Boston at the fringe of a complex of hospitals connected with the Harvard Medical School. The hospital is run jointly by Harvard and the State of Massachusetts with coterminous appointments and relatively great autonomy from traditional state hospital practices. The three demands on such a facility —*teaching, research,* and *service*—may at times be the focus of staff discussion, but there is general agreement that training needs are primary. Thus, the Director of Psychiatry annually includes in his welcoming remarks a statement that, "I do not expect you to cure anybody: just investigate, investigate, and learn, learn."

A pioneer of day hospitalizations, open doors, street clothes for staff, and other social innovations, the hospital has a daily census of about 200 patients, but perhaps a third of these are sleeping outside the hospital. The average stay in the hospital is 10 weeks and nearly 1000 individuals are admitted annually. About 2 per cent of admissions—the most uncontrollable, as a rule—are transferred to the more custodial state hospitals. The bulk of persons admitted become psychotherapy patients for first-year residents, who continue with 4 to 8 long-term patients beyond discharge and throughout the usual 3 years of training, while other patients become intermittent and short-term cases. Diagnostically, 31 per cent of inpatients are considered schizophrenic, while 10 per cent have affective psychotic disorders. Although psychoanalytically oriented psychotherapy is the major treatment modality, the psychotropic drugs, electroshock treatments, group psychotherapy, and experimental modalities such as mother and baby admissions in postpartum psychoses are employed where appropriate.

The hospital is administratively divided into four inpatient "services." Each service is located in a physically independent area and consists of 50 adult patients with its own resident, nursing, attendant, and occupational therapy staff. Six first-year residents start their training on the ward of each service the beginning of July. Responsibility is shared between a chief resident and a staff visit, the latter having several years of experience beyond his training. The supervised first-year resident is largely on his own with day-to-day encounters and decisions from his first week at the Psycho. His administrative superiors are available at daily service rounds and case presentations as well as at scheduled and unscheduled personal conferences. The resident rapidly discovers that the structure of the system is one which sacrifices tight control of therapeutic measures to promote early confrontation with the problems of independence, self-reliance, and competence.

The Task of Learning Psychotherapy

The resident's primary task during this first year will be to learn about treating psychotic patients in psychotherapy. The treatment task with the acute psychoses has been conceptualized by Semrad in the previous chapters as having three phases. First is the stage of restitution of ego function during which the patient is aided in his efforts to acknowledge, bear, and put into perspective the painful experiences which precipitated a psychotic reaction. The therapist's work consists of supplying in his relationship with the patient the emotional sustenance, support, and gratification necessary to allow the patient to give up the psychotic defense mechanisms by which he has been dealing with his pain. Second is a stage of maintenance of recompensation, during which the patient is aided in gaining a relatively comfortable and stable perspective on the precipitating experience which can persist internally without dependence on the therapist. Third is the stage of analysis of the psychosis-vulnerable ego, one in which work is devoted to understanding this vulnerability and substituting nonpsychotic for psychotic ways of dealing with stress. Identification with the therapist is of major importance in accomplishing these tasks. These three stages are lengthy, and since a resident can seldom work with any individual patient more than 2 years, supervisory work usually involves only the first two stages.

An intellectual grasp of the psychotherapy task may be easily achieved, but to understand it usefully, the resident must accumulate clinical experience, much as is true for learning the therapy tasks of other branches of medicine. Each case is approached as an investigation with three questions: What precipitated the illness? Why was that particular patient vulnerable to that particular stress? And why were psychotic mechanisms used in the reaction? Shortly the resident finds that the paths of his investigation lead in a great many directions and he is inundated with data which are hard to evaluate. Answers are further obscured by the patient's evasions and obstructions, with which the resident is unfamiliar and ill equipped to work, and by his own emotional reactions to his patient. As detailed in subsequent chapters, one of the supervisor's tasks will be to lend a helping hand, in whatever way required, to assist the resident in working through these obstructions and confusions toward the answers he seeks.

As this formulation of the patient's illness becomes clear, the nature of the psychotherapy task can be understood in specific terms, in terms of the individual patient's life experiences. It remains then to begin. However, doing so requires of the resident skills and knowledge which he has not sufficiently acquired and which can only be acquired in the course of attempting the work. The skill which forms the cornerstone of psychotherapeutic capacity is empathic understanding: that is, the ability to feel one's self into the patient in order to gain an understanding of what he is experiencing. Usually, the resident will begin with an intellectual recognition of, then a sympathetic involvement in his patient's life. He is able to stand off from his patient and exercise his intellect about him, but when he gets closer to the patient's affective experience, he tends to lose his intellectual moorings, falling in not only with his patient's feelings but also with his view of his life. As such, the resident loses the vantage point of his objectivity. Helping the resident to develop out of this raw material the refined capacity of empathic understanding is a major part of the supervisor's task.

The Background of the Beginning Psychiatric Resident

Even a cursory glance at our medical schools and internship programs reveals a culture in many important ways different from that of the teaching psychiatric hospital. For at least 5 years, the individual is carefully tutored in the tangible data of malfunctioning during the biological life cycle. He cultivates his fingers, eyes, and ears to discern murmurs and organ margins, nodules, and pigmented nevi. Further, he is taught to extend his senses with the use of test tubes, microscopes, electrocardiograms, and computers. The medical student has spent years building personal styles which remove the subjective from his observations, which sacrifice intuition and feeling to guarantee better the concurrence of objectively measurable phenomena with his immediate sense impressions.

Surgery and pathology have taught him how to view persons dispassionately, how to emphasize detail and with a limited focus serve the organ without emotional identification with the organism. Were empathy required, the blood and guts inherent in a medical education would be unbearable stresses for most students. Death has been mastered at the autopsy table, and the early squeamishness of the medical student has been supplanted by the bravado of the intern in the emergency room. Suppression and denial of personal feeling are fostered in these students.

Treatment of the nonpsychiatric patient relies on the physician's actions and on his manipulations. The prescription of pills or the use of the scalpel involve an acting *on* the sick person by the healer in a controlling way and depend on the scientific authority of the medical man. In the same respect, the great teachers of medicine, from Hippocrates and Galen through Vesalius to Osler, have been revered authorities whose words have been repeated by students and colleagues partly to fill the need for final, omnipotent figures amid the uncertainties of disease and death. Although current medical school pedagogy is in no wise as hierarchical as the Parisian hospital of Charcot's time, the inheritance of reverence for professional authority has to some extent been impersonalized by a pursuit of scientific truth in the laboratory and in the library.

A sense of responsibility has gradually developed in the new physician, and any uncertainty he might have in his medical knowledge may be suppressed as he trains himself for rapid and frequently effective responses to life-endangering situations. One of the most common questions the beginning psychiatrist asks after discussing an interview with his supervisor—and often after receiving some clarification of the dynamic significance of the interaction—is, "But what should I *do* now?"

Thus the reflex to respond to threatening affect or behavior by action has been reinforced during recent emergency room training, where extensive understanding as a crucial aspect of the physician's role has been necessarily devalued.

The heritage of medical tradition has crystallized in the mature resident a dual sense of obligation to the patient and of commitment to the discovery of scientific reality. The art of medicine lies in balancing investigations with actions according to the urgencies and circumstances of any given clinical situation. The methods of inquiry developed during medical school are fact-gathering explorations focusing on uncovering the disease process, the immediate implications of this process, and the therapy which stands the greatest chance of alleviating the patient's distress. Thus, an abdominal pain is approached with the assurance that information about its location (epigastric? right-lower quadrant?), duration, and quality will distinguish between the burst appendix demanding immediate laparotomy and the chronic gastritis which diet and antiacids will help to heal. But the exploration of medical history-taking always implies, "I do this scientific investigation in order to find a treatment procedure if such is possible." The inquiry, the clarification, the lab tests go as far as reasonably indicated to determine the physicians' action, and thus investigation remains as a kind of preliminary to the physician's *real* service which is to reduce the patient's suffering.

Psychotherapy stands in contrast. Primary in therapy is investigation.[1] Whatever is revealed by history-taking may bear on decisions about medication and ward privileges, but the means of general medicine become both means and ends in psychiatry. The beginning psychiatric resident must give up the personal gratification obtained when his medical actions produced lessening of physical suffering and find satisfaction in relentlessly investigating, in comprehending more completely, and in accepting his own silent participation as one of his major therapeutic tools. Delay of impulse gratification is demanded in the earliest as well as in later phases of treatment.

That part of the medical identity which relies on satisfaction of the need to heal must be suspended if the bright intern is to become a patient psychotherapist who waits for a conflict to crystallize in its dynamic significance before attempting interpretation. There is a need for appropriate action (usually of a sustaining or supporting variety) in the treatment of psychotic people, but it is only within a well-balanced context of investigation and interpersonal concern.

The interdisciplinary relationships of the general hospital are developed with concentration of responsibility in the person and mystique of the physician. A nurse or a lab technician obey, they carry out orders, and they participate in a team which has clearly defined expectation, modes of communication, and chain of command. Although the intern found himself a novice among his medical colleagues, the rest of the hospital employees endowed him with the respect of his medical position and even a veteran nurse must finally acquiesce to his decisions.

Before he starts his residency, the new psychiatrist has suppressed his instinctual life and advanced in his medical career by minimizing his feelings, relying on personal and scientific authorities, employing complex instruments to further his senses, and resorting to action in the face of uncertainty. The tasks implicit in his development into a therapist of psychotic persons—to understand empathically, structure relationships cooperatively, use himself as the instrument of observation and treatment, and tolerate psychic conflict—demand significant adaptations of the beginning resident's personality.

THE IDENTITY CRISIS OF THE BEGINNING PSYCHIATRIC RESIDENT

On entering the Massachusetts Mental Health Center, the resident begins to pursue a new professional identity. Clearly, the ego ideals of recent years become inappropriate, for adaptive as they were in the general hospital or laboratory, they are at odds with the flexibility and sensitivity required if the physician is to become a competent psychiatrist. Fantasies of new professional heroes abound at this time and they range from that of the silent but omniscient psychoanalyst to the aggressive and masterful administrator.[2] He will become like the professor from medical school whose lectures and Freudian interpretations excited his curiosity in unconscious processes. Or he will be more attuned to sociological theories and apply these to his ward to vindicate an instructor from college.

We view the first several months of training as being ones of inevitable confusion and anxiety—as a crisis in professional identity formation—while the resident sorts out those elements of his earlier medical experience (such as his thirst for empirical data and his sense of medical responsibility) which are coherent with this new and strange setting. Personal psychic determinants have led the resident to choose this medical specialty, and such unconscious factors as unresolved omnipotent feelings produce an irrational and relatively obscured set of private needs and expectations within each new psychiatrist. His search for answers has brought him here (to a psychiatric hospital) supposedly to work with disturbed persons who in no way resemble him in their problems, but his desire to cure his own psyche is not so irrelevant. Thus, a profession or a specialty is selected for mastery partly because it is a feared area of danger or disease, and the resident has unwittingly acknowledged in making his decision to enter psychiatry that he is challenged by irrational behavior. The discovery that the reality of treating psychotic patients contains more threats of disquietude than promises of understanding, that tolerance for affective interchanges is only painfully developed, and that it will be many months before the beginner is relatively relaxed in his work—these discoveries produce a series of personal conflicts which may be viewed as the primary hurdle in the mastery of the new specialty. The resident is confronted with extreme tensions and boredom during his early weeks as an actual psychiatrist, and his fantasies of what it would be like to be a psychiatrist are found to be just as inadequate as were his attempts to imitate earlier medical heroes. In a state of limbo, he looks backwards and forwards to find his path out of the vicissitudes of his new role.

Erikson has considered the crisis occurring during identity development, and his discussion of *Young Man Luther*[3] is certainly appropriate to the dilemma of the beginning psychiatric resident. The quest for a secure role and certain self is confounded by the environment's expectation that he possess capacities of empathic understanding and behavioral observation which he has not yet developed. Gerald Caplan[4] has further examined developmental crises, and in his concern with the patterns of life crises has indicated some of the directions pathology may take and the manner in which institutional anticipation may have a preventive effect. The resident must give up much of the confidence recently earned in the general hospital and gain perspective on himself as an unskilled beginner who in fact knows very little when he acts as a psychotherapist. To achieve a new professional identity, he must mourn his systematized and controlling styles painstakingly developed over recent years, must suffer tension and depression, and must struggle to comprehend the unknown inside himself as well as what is around him and his patients. In the middle of this adjustment, turmoil, fixation, regression, and maturation are all likely and may be seen at differing times in varying degrees in each new resident. The hospital, however, provides supports as well as challenges and the sources of strength around the resident are important determinants in the outcome of this critical period.

The Hospital and the Resident

In other chapters discussing the resident's development, we will be primarily concerned with individual supervision as it may reflect the vicissitudes of growth and as it may catalyze maturation. A teaching institution must be self-conscious of its entire being. We recognize innumerable "incidental" aspects of our hospital (such as a coffee shop staffed by patients or a salary paid by the Commonwealth of Massachusetts) which have an impact upon our training program. Although it is not our purpose to detail these aspects of the environment in which the resident grows, some of the ingredients of our fertile soil deserve brief consideration.

On the ward, the resident finds social workers, nurses, and other professionals with years of experience treating psychiatric patients and he—the greenest of them all—expects to write the prescription which they will deferentially follow, for so it has been for the physician elsewhere. Initial attempts at teamwork often become the old and familiar, the authoritarian relationship of the surgeon with the scrub nurse. For example, one anxious resident appeared on the ward Sundays and holidays and phoned in the middle of the night to ascertain whether the orders he had written for tranquilizers were being utilized to calm his disturbed patient. We view such events as a preservation of a previous, secure identity, and we suggest that these phenomena are symptoms of the crisis in identity formation. The flexibility of the hospital system can tolerate such incidents and thus help the newcomer maintain his self-esteem as he evolves toward more appropriate relationships. On the ward, habitual patterns are scrutinized in the setting of service rounds, and the new resident finds that other beginners have similar uncertainties.

Administrative actions must always be integrated with psychodynamic understanding if a hospital is to nurture therapy with disturbed patients. Again and again the young resident is threatened by a person whose feelings are out of control (the raging paranoid, the self-mutilating wrist-slasher, or the disrobing temptress) and decisions about limit-setting may be made by a green doctor in a near panic state. Retaliative, provocative, and blandly denying orders appear on the patient's chart, and obviously a vital area of professional growth is the development of skill in assessing the patient's needs and realities while bearing in mind the availabilities and limitations of the ward situation. The decisions reached around restriction, medication, and overall ward management are those of the resident treating the patient, but he is in day-to-day touch with senior physicians who evaluate, discuss, and if necessary countermand administrative steps. The chief resident and the staff visit have responsibility for the care of the patients, and much of the teaching of "how to administrate" becomes a direct offering of themselves for imitation. Since residents do act out their feelings about patients, these teachers are in a position to set limits on the beginner in an empathic way (firmly insisting on attendance at conferences or reminding about paperwork chores) and to help him bear his distressing feelings. At such times, a chief resident will tell a resident to "take this up with your supervisor" and this becomes a frequent way to stem acting out and to accent thinking through. Just as the resident learns to supplant action by careful consideration so he may impart the same emphasis on delay of action to his patients.

The psychiatrist customarily acts as an auxiliary ego for disturbed patients in two manners: he limits motility and he encourages investigation of interpersonal and intrapsychic conflict. Occasionally, a therapist-administrator split in function is arranged for very difficult manic or hyperactive borderline patients using two first-year residents. With the functions disentangled, the resident may better grasp the intricacies of becoming a psychiatrist. Part of the value of this approach is that the resident gains a comprehension of the problems in limit-setting his counterpart now faces. When effective it leads to more rapid internalization of the methods of the ward administrators who may otherwise become distorted as rigid, arbitrary, and feelingless authorities. Recent consideration of such therapeutic-administrative splits[5] raises important ques-

tions about their impact on the length of patients' hospitaliza-
tion but do not detract from their usefulness in teaching
beginners.

Peer relations do play a significant part in aiding individuals through this developmental period. Residents have constant opportunities to observe their fellows at their best and
worst and to learn from the mistakes of others. The stumbling
or frantic approaches of fellow residents can be weighed and
warmly probed with a senior person present to clarify common
problems and to catalyze discussion. The study of group processes through group participation is often utilized for the
common expression of dissatisfaction, distaste for the hospital
administration, and projects to reform the institution. The inclination to cement working friendships into social ones is
strong and many of the inherent rivalries are buried in communal entertaining such as ward parties. Each Christmas, the
first-year residents present a play which primarily satirizes the
qualities of the senior staff. Thus, there is safety within the
group for the manifestation of negative feelings about these
ambivalent objects of painful growth.

Formal pedagogical exercises (lectures, seminars, and assigned literature) are another avenue for finding out what it is
like to be a psychotherapist. These, however appeal to the intellect, not to the preconscious self which builds ego-ideals,
and although needed in the total residency training program
they do not dislodge the substratum of medical approaches
developed over prior years. In fact they may reinforce scho-
lasticism and emotional isolation. Residents may emphasize
the printed textbook to avoid the disturbed patient whose behavior and verbalizations are too threatening to be accepted
as communications of one human being to another.

> One beginner repeatedly took issue with the diagnoses staff
> members suggested for schizophrenic patients. Was this a
> paranoid state or was it paranoia? He could quote noso-

logical definitions, yet the preoccupation was serving to defer his appreciation of the emptiness and emotional chaos of his patients' lives.

Such a need to classify may be a necessary way-station for the newcomer as he struggles to comprehend those experiences which so baffle the colleagues he left in the general hospital. Although formal teaching may help bind the resident's early anxiety into familiar paths of knowledge, the danger exists that a resident will flee from his primary task of learning about psychotherapy with his patients and embrace intellectual challenges as safe substitutes.

With corridors of social and biological scientists nearby, some residents are diverted by interests in research laboratories. Earlier pursuits such as medical school research projects or even college theses are revived, and the dusty biochemical formulas are reviewed for pertinence to the enigmas of schizophrenia. Careers may be shaped by just such amalgams, at times catalyzed by government appointments and grants, and the individual develops an area of competence built upon prior successful mastery of challenges which help lessen the sense of current inadequacy. However, when early involvement of the beginner in research is an avoidance of doctor-patient immediacies it can be very detrimental to the professional maturation of the individual.

The senior psychiatric staff at the "Psycho" present yet another combination of opportunity and danger.[6] By the fact of their ages, experiences, and positions, they are revered and endowed with knowledge and power beyond the reality. Legends abound; charisma develops, and environmentally supported idealized images are available. Many of the nebulous fantasies of what it would be like to be a psychiatrist are projected on to the persons of the professors. In an institution where conflicting goals exist and are often embodied in different persons, the resident may meet a "triple-threat" temptation by setting his ambitions at becoming a wise therapist, a powerful administrator, and a renowned investigator—all at once. Such exaggerations of an individual's potential help to deny the sense of weakness otherwise permeating these first months. The senior staff is available to permit residents to check out their preconceptions and to unmask the men behind the myths. Case presentations, patient interviews, and encounters over coffee are antidotes to unrealistic idealization, since they provide opportunity for observation of seasoned professional styles in action.

There are innumerable varieties of regressive responses to the stresses on the beginner and a subsequent chapter will discuss these defensive actions more fully. Examples include the resident who picks up an ophthalmoscope after his patient complains of her eyes hurting, or the urging on a patient of rapid decisions when the patient has been in long-standing conflict. In such situations, the institutional forces are relatively peripheral to the central focus of the resident's struggle as he searches for his new identity in his new situation. At this stage in his career, one can expect the resident to be trying on a series of borrowed and patched vestments, and he requires a mirror as well as a tailor to help him decide which fits for what occasion. It is our contention that the supervisor who individually works with the first-year resident as he learns the therapy of psychotic patients can fill precisely that role.

THE SUPERVISOR AND THE RESIDENT

The gross inexperience of the beginning resident is the unspoken point of initiation of all supervision. Eager for structure, floundering in the unfamiliar territory of feeling, concerned lest his inadequacy be criticized or injure his patients, his first fumbling steps plea for help—denials and insistences notwithstanding. His determination to cure the chronic psychotic, to comprehend the unfathomable—his rescue fantasies —provide a zeal which often outdoes the seasoned therapist and supervisor and which can become the core of his motivation for learning to be a psychotherapist. He submits to the discipline of the psychiatric residency and to its vital supervisory relationships with much ambivalence about his own potential. Introduction to supervision must include a channeling of these drives to mastery into the acquiring of essential skills. The desire to cure is met by a demand from the supervisor that the beginner investigate. The resident's powers of observation must become sharper so that a smile or giggle is perceived in its affective context and takes on meaning in the larger context of the patient's situation. A mental status examination comes to life as an assessment of psychic functioning, for the supervisee soon discovers that his interviewing techniques must serve him with the psychotic patient as once his instruments and laboratory values helped him to follow the progress of his medical patients. One of the early communications of supervision is an implicit, "You don't know much about therapy, but I can help you to learn something about what's going on as you struggle to treat this patient." When the resident begins to appreciate this gap of experience, he has begun supervision. He can then become constructively involved in the process, for even though the fantasies and resistances around becoming a therapist will continue to complicate his professional growth they are now open for discussion.

In his weekly meeting with his supervisor during this first year, the resident is reviewing the process of treatment as it is occurring with one or more psychotic patients. Administrative responsibility is clearly left to the staff of the ward, from which the supervisor usually remains discrete, and where conflicting recommendations have developed in supervision, it is up to the resident to discuss these with his chief resident and his staff-visit. The resident is not an intermediary in a chain of supervisor-resident-patient, although this is a common fantasy and some teachers acknowledge such an approach. Where ultimate responsibility rests with the supervisor we find residents become involved unnecessarily in power struggles which greatly hamper the collaborative aspects of a supervisory relationship. He may act out by omitting written orders, subvert the work of the nurses, or juggle medicines. Such rebellions and compliances are inevitable concomitants of the development of a professional identity and will occur in various hospital relationships, but supervision can be so arranged as to be as free as possible of opportunities to act out authoritarian conflicts. Less responsible for "service"—neither to the welfare of the patient nor to the well-being of the ward community—the supervisor can place his emphasis on the resident's development as a therapist. In essence, a teaching-administrative split is in operation. The supervisor can pay attention to the issues this individual presents as he evolves from a medical man into a psychiatrist. The supervisor can consider the therapist's evasions or manipulations as doctor and patient size each other up, and his curiosity about that diadic relationship can be the model for the resident's own therapeutic investigation of the patient's life. His stance with the resident—learning with him, rather than teaching to him—provides the opportunity for what may be a novel relationship and the prototype of effective psychotherapy: the doctor who works along with his patient without acting on him.

Indeed, the supervisor is working to structure a situation which will maximize the learning of the resident. In this sense he is calling on the best of the beginner to face the intricate material of life experience and to develop as consciously as possible a way of ordering its senselessness. Initially, it may be most appropriate for the supervisor to openly display his own style and intuitions about a given patient, to discuss the thinking which leads to concern over suicide or a freedom from that concern. This would be a direct offering by the supervisor of his own psychiatric ways, of a part of the supervisor's professional identity. But the supervisor uses most of his effort in encouraging the resident to find personally appropriate identifications: he may question, he may suggest, he may relay his own discoveries, or he may tell parables—but his objective is to promote growth rather than to convey an ordered body of knowledge.

Supervision must be distinguished from psychotherapy. The supervisor works as a part of a training institution and is concerned with aspects of personality which interfere with professional growth, while no restrictions on the scope of legitimate interest are put on the psychotherapist. The initial year of psychiatric residency often contains other highly significant life events (marriage, birth of children, death of parents), and the supervisor suspects their impact on the beginner's work without sanction to explore their nature. The individual entering psychotherapy for himself—and at one time or another most of our residents do so—is making his entire life experience available for discussion, while the supervisor can only work with the data of a few carefully delimited relationships. In sounding out the role of the supervisor, the beginner may see supervision and therapy interchangeably, and some residents attempt to "bootleg" therapy by bringing personal concerns which are irrelevant to their patients into supervision. The alert supervisor may recognize this as a misunderstanding, as an evasion of some more painful material in the resident's treatment of a patient, or as a tacit plea for referral to an appropriate analyst or therapist.

The beginning resident is once again seeking to obtain the credentials possessed by a more experienced group of men. As a recapitulation of oedipal struggles, this period also requires that positive identifications occur if the first-year resident is to develop the diagnostic skills and empathic understanding crucial to the task of psychotherapy. This process can be expedited or impeded by early, meaningful supervisory contacts. The supervisor is bringing a host of life experiences to supervision which in some ways parallel the resident's current conflicts and disappointments. The supervisor can interpolate these both supportively and creatively in the interest of making himself visible as a person who has survived the crisis of identity formation and who is ready to lend his style to a younger colleague now struggling to develop one of his own. The supervisor's assessments and understanding of the resident's difficulties can become the foundation for the resident of what will be a life-long growth of psychotherapeutic competence.

REFERENCES

1. Semrad, Elvin V.: Long-term therapy of schizophrenia. In: Usdin, Gene I. (Ed.): Psychoneurosis and Schizophrenia. Philadelphia, J. B. Lippincott Company, 1966, pp. 155–173.
2. Sharaf, Myron R., and Levinson, Daniel J.: The quest for omnipotence in professional training. Psychiatry 27:135–149, 1964.
3. Erikson, Erik H.: Young Man Luther; A Study in Psychoanalysis and History. New York, W. W. Norton, 1958.
4. Caplan, Gerald: Principles of Preventive Psychiatry. New York, Basic Books, 1964.
5. Beck, James C., Macht, Lee B., Levinson, Daniel J., and Strauss, Milton: A controlled experimental study of the therapist-administrator split. Amer. J. Psychiat. 124:467–474, 1967.
6. Hodgson, Richard C.: Role Relations in an Executive Group. Unpublished doctoral dissertation, Graduate School of Business Administration, Harvard University, 1963.

CHAPTER V

The Work of Supervision

By John T. Maltsberger, M.D. and
Dan H. Buie, Jr., M.D.

The work of the supervisor requires a basis for conceptualization which does not neatly fit our accustomed diagnostic or descriptive phrases. Between the inadequacies of the beginner, the competency of the teacher, and the process of identification we would interpolate a framework orienting the supervisor. As is so often the case, much of our thinking has crystallized around the discussion of particular examples, and we recognize that although good supervision may be done without an intellectual grasp of the principles of supervision, the potential for the most effective use of the teacher's talents can only be developed as hunches are abandoned in favor of hypotheses, as data is gathered to test such hypotheses of pedagogy, and as supervision of psychotherapy can be approached as a science. Again, psychodynamic psychiatry offers an example of an art shedding its magical coloration to become a science retaining an essence of humanism. Much the same can be done for the understanding of supervision; insofar as its effectiveness has, or does, depend upon the mystique or authority or pretended omniscience of a given teacher, the apprentice is being exposed to a mysterious process while pursuing a supposedly scientific profession.

Successful supervision demands the establishment of a *supervisory alliance*. Teacher and student must feel a mutual commitment to the task of helping the student work with his patients no matter what these persons may present or evoke in the resident. The motto "Nothing human is alien to me" reflects such a capacity to bear distressing feeling and to shun flight or avoidance in favor of a determination to understand. The good supervisory alliance is built over time and with obstacles serving not just as detours but as potentially productive byways. Much of the work of the supervisor must focus on just this alliance. He must exercise those aspects of his professional self which will strengthen that alliance, recognizing that the vicissitudes of the identification process may lead to exaggerated imitation or to deliberate defiance.

There are many stones in the road which impede progress toward the goals we have outlined. The first clinical encounters with psychotic patients are notorious for their stresses. With colleagues we may eventually share stories of the inward commotions and the blunders associated with these first confrontations; sometimes as time passes and skill increases, they shrink to grounds for friendly teasing. The fear, hopelessness, guilt, arousal, and rage evoked in these early encounters is diminished in memory with the accumulation of experience. A highly empathic attitude is required to estimate the distress of a resident who is just beginning his work.

The essence of the supervisor's work is to diagnose what the resident needs in order to treat his patient and to supply what is needed by the resident. Diagnosis of the need requires as a first step gaining an understanding of *areas of interference* which are preventing a resident from doing his therapy. Second, the supervisor must discover what *defense mechanisms* are used by the resident in connection with such an area. Finally, he must determine the *supervisory maneuver* appropriate to the distress of the resident in the light of the interference and the defense. Such a formulation is ongoing and constantly subject to revision, but it is the rational basis for the response a supervisor can then make, a response of sustenance, support, or gratification. As the supervisor supplies the learning needs of the resident, identification with the teacher will proceed.

AREAS OF INTERFERENCE

Review of our experience has led us to recognize six broad areas where we see interference in the resident's current functioning as a therapist. These overlap, but a specific problem in the course of therapy must be delineated as to where it most clearly falls. Errors in a supervisor's judgment on this basic point will show up in subsequent work. Where a teaching intervention has been based on a false premise, a therapist's interpretations and responses to his patient will appear as misdirected. In some respects, such areas are the apparent manifestations of unmastered aspects of being a psychotherapist.

1. Personal Emotional
    Burdens

Not all interferences are relevant to the ongoing process of learning or growing as a psychiatrist. Residents will suffer setbacks in their personal lives unrelated to their work with patients which can produce unbearable feelings and become severe impediments to work as a psychotherapist. When residents are overwhelmed, preoccupied, or depressed by stresses (such as the fears of being drafted or the death of family members), their capacity to utilize supervision is limited. Some may actually depersonalize; some may become depressed. The alert supervisor will discuss such problems only as essential to a patient's welfare and will support a resident's desire to seek personal therapy to deal with nonprofessional problems. There is a range of such instances with one extreme being that of established personality patterns acting as interferences. These may be evident at first and sometimes are more readily worked with in supervision, but sometimes they require direct confrontation as well as recommendations for analytic treatment.

> A resident had treated three paranoid patients with similar failures in each instance: the patient would become violent, run away, or provoke transfer to a closed hospital. Repeated discussions by the supervisor were ineffective. The supervisor noted this pattern, began focusing on the anger this resident's patients could not express in therapy hours, and as the supervisor did so the beginner became markedly anxious. When the beginner recognized his limitations in bearing aggressive feelings with his patients, he verbalized connections with his personal life and then asked his supervisor for a referral to an analyst.

2. Ignorance and
Inexperience

Several areas of ignorance and inexperience may require a supervisor's helpful intervention. A resident sometimes needs assistance in learning how to keep his patient talking about relevant details and how to formulate hypotheses actively during the interview, testing them on the spot by eliciting pertinent responses from his patient. He may need help in organizing his data so to gain the most understanding of his patient's life, seeing the emotional meanings of events and behaviors and being able to recognize the important unknown areas yet to be delineated. At times a resident, at a loss for a more effective method, will revert to using procedures learned in the medical or surgical clinics, as one resident did when he responded to his patient's symbolic complaints about her ear by immediate otoscopic examination. When a resident has not yet developed sufficient ego capacity to tolerate his patient's intense affects and impulses, he may require help from his supervisor to do so. He may signal his need for this help in a number of ways: appearing overtly anxious, diverting so much energy to handling the affect that he cannot think effectively about what is going on, adopting defensively a business-like attitude, setting limits impulsively, becoming angry and rejecting toward his patient, recognizing but neglecting the threatening affective material, or denying the existence or extent of the affect. From inexperience and ignorance a resident can proceed to a sense of inadequacy, especially when faced with a series of difficult patients. As a result he might defer to the advice of nursing personnel even when it is contrary to his own judgment, become overly fearful of staff criticism, or become defensively defiant towards constructive suggestions. Similar attitudes would then develop with his patients.

3. Need for Omnipotence and Omniscience

A resident's need to fulfill a narcissistically determined ideal image of himself can be a force to be directed toward professional growth or it can be an impediment. Professional growth is possible as an outcome when this narcissistic need is manifested in relation to the supervisor and becomes worked through in a creative identification process. When expressed as part of his work with patients, the result carries no benefit except as the resident might be able to learn from errors made at the patient's expense. Most commonly the problem arises when the resident believes his competency is measured in accordance with his capacity to control his patients' lives. Their successes have become his successes, their failures his failures. And so his self-esteem is continually vulnerable to the inevitable fluctuations in a patient's clinical state. A resident might thus feel that regressions in his patients are insulting, negative responses to his therapeutic efforts. Unrealistic rescue fantasies are another form of this narcissistic need, and they are sometimes intensified when there has been a previous psychotherapist—especially one more senior—on the case, or a resident believes that psychodynamic forces can be controlled by some form, subtle or gross, of fiat. He might be overtly directive in interviews, or he might even try to control a patient's upsurge of destructive impulses by commands and threats. Yet another form of the problem is the need to be seen as very accomplished and capable by the patient. This may lead to various forms of showing off: by means of multiple, premature interpretations, displays of educational background, or even frank bragging. Whatever form the need for omnipotence and omniscience might take, self-devaluation, angry devaluation of the patient, and guilt are the end products. When a resident's low self-esteem is the product of the inevitable disappointment of primitive and distorted expectations of himself, he becomes vulnerable to his patients' efforts to attack him by devaluation.

4.   Distress with Instincts

Psychotic patients present intense stimuli to those who spend much time with them. For the resident, sitting with them hour after hour has the effect of a sustained assault on his defenses, to the point that his own sexual and aggressive impulses threaten or actually break through to conscious awareness. He may feel himself vulnerable to his patient's conscious or unconscious seductiveness and might find himself responding with some degree of seductiveness on his own part. Much the same kind of thing can occur with aggressive impulses. Anxiety, rejection of the patient, or guilt are likely to ensue.

5.   Countertransference

We use this term in its narrowest sense, as defined by Annie Reich.[1] As such we have considered countertransference to be the effect of the psychotherapist's *unconscious needs and conflicts* on his understanding of the patient and on his therapeutic efforts. It can occur in two forms; one arises when the patient represents an object from the therapist's past on to whom past feelings and impulses are displaced; the other arises when the activity or situation of psychotherapy holds an unconscious meaning for the therapist which is put into action.

Countertransference is considerably more likely to interfere with the psychotherapeutic efforts of the beginner than it is with the work of an experienced therapist. The resident is also less likely to recognize the signs of countertransference, and when he does, he is inclined to embarrassed reticence about it with his supervisor. He may even be frankly fearful of his supervisor's discovering it.

6. Relative Inability to Understand Empathically

This problem will receive attention in a subsequent section, in which the tendency of a beginner to lose objectivity with his patient by inappropriate projections and introjections will be described, along with various devices utilized to avoid experiencing the patient's feelings and impulses. The resident's effectiveness is limited by subjective responses which, although often nonverbal in nature, could be stated as follows: "I am very much like him," "He is very much like me," "I feel his distress and will comfort him," "I can see what he is talking about, but I have no experience like it," and "Whatever he is talking about makes no sense; it's completely psychotic." As the resident gains experience his capacity for empathy will grow to be one which could be verbalized as "I have had experiences similar to his which I have mastered but retained in memory, and on the basis of these I can imagine myself into his life situation and understand both how he feels and why he feels what he does."

DEFENSE MECHANISMS AND INTERFERENCES WITH LEARNING

An assessment of a problem in supervision first arrives at a diagnosis of the area of interference. The next task the supervisor approaches is that of determining which defense mechanisms are being unconsciously employed in the resident's struggle to persist with therapy in spite of that interference. The obstruction to the progress of treatment can only be relieved as the nature of the resident's needs and his reactions to these needs are clarified and met by supervisory maneuvers.

Inevitably the normal defensive patterns which are employed in everyday life are called into play when a young physician is confronted with a threatening psychotic patient for the first time. It should not surprise us that neurotic defensive patterns will also appear. A moment's reflection on the history of psychiatry recalls that the greater number of men have always responded to these troubling patients by flight or something worse, and it is not remarkable that the beginner tends to shrink away and avoid much of what confronts him, resolute as he may be to learn how to treat psychotic patients psychotherapeutically. The work of supervision must concern itself with the operations of the apprentice's defensive apparatus if the task is to be done; natural and universal as they may be in everyday life, where they are useful in the avoidance of painful affect, these patterns of reaction operate in the clinical situation to obscure from the therapist exactly what is going on with his patient. It is the function of the defensive patterns to keep out of awareness those very affects and impulses which the psychotic patient displays undisguisedly; the beginner does not acknowledge kinship to psychosis without pain. He tries to avoid it and requires the assistance of an empathic supervisor in order to acknowledge, bear, and put into perspective his reactions to the clinical situation.

Psychotherapy of psychosis, like psychotherapy with dying patients, generates guilt, anxiety, anger, and other painful affects. Defenses against such feelings may considerably diminish the usefulness of the therapist for his patient. Norton, in her significant and valuable report of the treatment of a dying patient, remarks:

> I was aware of grief, guilt, anxiety, and anger during this (final) hour, but I am sure it is apparent that defenses against any of these countertransference responses, whether denial, reassurance, repression, overprotectiveness, false optimism, or intellectualization, would have markedly interfered with my usefulness to the patient as the object she needed. My conscious awareness of the sources of these responses was what made it possible for me to respond appropriately in terms of her needs. In essence, the dying patient inevitably provokes countertransference responses in the analyst, but acceptance and utilization of these can be most therapeutic for the patient.[2]

Residents are relatively mature individuals. Generally the defensive mechanisms they use are those more typically employed in normals: repression, isolation, displacement, rationalization, etc. These are the mechanisms which were developed to manage threats arising from within in the form of impulses and associated affects. However, when sitting and talking with an intensely frightening or stimulating patient, threats arise from both within and without. The patient becomes an objective source of anxiety, and at the same time, impulses and other affects are aroused against which the usual defenses may be insufficient. The developmentally more primitive mechanisms, denial, distortion, and projection, must then be mobilized.

Denial* is employed both against threatening external

---

* A more complete description of denial can be synthesized from many sources in the literature. Drawing on Anna Freud,[3] Edward Bibring and Arthur Valenstein (Bibring et al.[4]), Edith Jacobson,[5] and Bertram Lewin,[6] the following statements can be made: Denial is a negation of conscious awareness which is directed against external

realities and against those threatening internal realities where repression is no longer effective. Not infrequently residents use denial in the service of protecting defenses of a neurotic type.

> One resident used denial to avoid a feeling response to his patient's graphic, intensely anxiety-laden recounting of cutting his throat in order to kill himself. The resident re-told the story to his supervisor in a business-like way as if it were a manual act of no particular consequence. Information also emerged about the resident which made it possible for his supervisor to understand his need to deny the affect in order to protect his own defense of isolation which was directed against the feelings associated with his own longstanding, once actively considered, self-destructive tendencies. The supervisor could see that this was an interference in the area of countertransference with a use of denial as a defense to maintain the therapist's equilibrium.

Projection is used by the resident as a means of disclaiming unacceptable attitudes, impulses and feelings toward himself or his patient by attributing them to another person, usually the patient. This provides justification for expressing toward the recipient of the projection some form of the otherwise unacceptable attitude, impulse, or feeling.

> A resident had little tolerance for hostility because he himself was by nature easily provoked to seething anger. Early in training he told his supervisor of his apprehension

---

reality and that part of internal reality which has laid claim on the ego for conscious recognition. While denial as a mechanism operates unconsciously, it cannot effect unconsciousness of that which is denied; it can at best only maintain the denied experience at the preconscious level. Denial may be directed selectively toward components of inner or outer reality: that is, an event, portion of an event, an idea, an impulse response, or an affect response. It may be effected in a pure form or through the collaboration of fantasy, word and act, exaggeration, or displacement.

about this aspect of his personality. One of his patients was a furious young woman who was continually in a rage with him and threatened suicide when frustrated. He responded with an unabating anger, guilt, and a fear that he could no longer tolerate the experience. At the same time he became convinced that his patient was not only sick but also "bad" and unchangeable. By projection of his own guilt and hopelessness about himself he was unconsciously trying to justify his wish to be rid of her. He would discharge her to another hospital whose function it is to care for the chronically ill. The supervisor's use of sustaining and supporting maneuvers enabled the resident to continue working with the patient. She resumed her former work, was discharged within a few months, and continued therapy as an outpatient.

It will be noted that these more primitive defenses are the ones employed most by psychotic patients. In their day-to-day lives, residents use them little; however, in the context of experiencing extreme emotion with their patients, they too are likely to fall back on denial and projection. It is the supervisor's task to include in his diagnosis the defensive maneuvers the resident is using in regard to his patient and the purposes being served thereby.

Supervisory Maneuvers

Having achieved a formulation of the area of interference and of the defense mechanism operating to impede treatment, the supervisor must determine what kind of supervisory activity is required to supply the therapist's needs and thus establish ongoing treatment. The complicated evaluation of interferences and defenses only points to the need for supervisory activity in a general way; the specific need for a maneuver is dictated by assessing the quality and intensity of the painful affect which threatens the resident. Avoidances can be abandoned, treatment can proceed, and learning can resume when the appropriate assistance is provided for dealing with the distress being generated in the therapist-patient relationship. Many sessions with the supervisor may be necessary before some of the self-protective but patient-alienating attitudes are replaced with psychotherapeutic ones. The context of activity by the supervisor, of words or actions which meet the present needs of the supervisee, becomes the matrix for the process of identification. *Sustaining maneuvers* are those efforts necessary to preserve the relationship between the apprentice and his patient. Without intervention of this kind the therapeutic effort will either collapse or be abandoned; a beginner requires this kind of assistance in order to persevere in his task. The supervisor bears some of the weight of the task, buoys up the therapeutic effort, and keep it from sinking away. The second class of supervisory efforts are the *supporting maneuvers,* through which the inherent potential of the beginner to serve his patient in a therapeutic way is developed and enhanced. Sustaining maneuvers are designed to maintain the matrix in which psychotherapy occurs, the therapeutic relationship. Supporting maneuvers presuppose the intactness of this matrix, and are specifically directed to help the resident proceed in a useful way; they enable him to develop and put to use his potential for healing. The remaining class of activities we call the *gratification maneuvers.* These refer to the supervisor's passive role once the beginner has developed his own capacity to persevere and makes use of the supervisor in working therapeutically. The therapist proceeds spontaneously to discover for himself new and useful ways of understanding and helping. This kind of supervisory work is gratification for the beginner in the sense that it represents a recompense for the effort his work requires—the satisfaction and pleasure of his own creative activity, recognized, respected, and acknowledged as such by his senior colleague. These maneuvers are of course parallel to those the resident uses with his patients. They are of fundamental importance in understanding the expression and fulfillment of interpersonal needs in all situations.

Sustaining Maneuvers

When the apprentice feels himself seriously slipping and failing in his efforts with a patient, there is a typical rise in anxiety. He feels helpless, impotent, and without help cannot proceed unless he can find means of flight from the stress at hand. If this flight is to be avoided the supervisor must intervene; when the supervisee is feeling overwhelmed, the intervention will most typically be by way of a *sustaining maneuver*. These particular supervisory efforts require more activity from the supervisor than others; they are by way of crisis interventions to prevent the combined distress of the patient and apprentice from capsizing the psychotherapeutic effort. It is at such moments as these that the beginner particularly needs to know that he has a resource to whom he can turn.

The importance of the supervisor's investment in helping the learner is particularly great at these moments. He must not only be able to correctly gauge what is happening in the therapy, and how distressed his apprentice is, but he must also care enough to be available quickly and willingly. The consolidation of a supervisory alliance often takes place when the supervisor is ready and willing to sustain in an emergency.

> One Saturday afternoon, a first-year resident found himself with a young woman patient who was threatening him with suicide. He telephoned his supervisor but was unable to reach him. A short while later the supervisor telephoned the hospital to say that he had received the message and would wait for a period of time at the telephone booth from which he was calling while the hospital operator tried to find the resident. Other seniors had intervened in the interval to assist in the crisis, and although resident and supervisor did not speak together until the next day, the investment which the supervisor showed in trying to help his apprentice greatly facilitated and enriched the supervisory work over the ensuing months.

First among the sustaining maneuvers is *to show a resident how to proceed.* Most typically this is to demonstrate to the resident, in an actual interview with his patient while he looks on, how to proceed in a therapeutic way. This kind of showing how is the most active and extreme of the sustaining techniques, and though typical of its class, is perhaps the one used least frequently.

> A beginning resident had been assigned to work with a middle-aged man who had come into the hospital with a severe depression. The symptom had not improved as the days passed, and one day, after a painful and unprofitable session with his patient, the therapist knocked on the door of his supervisor in an obvious state of distress. It soon became clear that the resident, like the patient, was turning his anger in upon himself, and felt completely unable to proceed further. The supervisor was able to interrupt what he was doing, and with the resident he returned to the ward, where the two of them talked with the patient together. The depressed man had recently lost his home due to a mortgage foreclosure. The supervisor inquired about the house, its history, its purchase, and demonstrated by interviewing how the necessary grieving could be promoted. The resident was greatly relieved now that he knew how to proceed and was able to continue with the patient.

Somewhat less direct and less active than showing how, but similar in purpose, is *to tell a resident how to proceed*. This is usually sufficient and, of course, is more commonly employed. Telling how is more appropriate in a situation when the apprentice is less distressed and can make use of this kind of communication.

> A patient had become depressed some 2 years previous to his admission shortly after the death of a congenitally crippled daughter. The resident had worked with the patient over the loss of his child for a month, but the patient had not really improved clinically, and the situation was becoming increasingly distressing. The supervisor was able to point out that it was not only the loss of the child that was troubling the patient, but further the question of who was

responsible for her death. The patient had been preoccupied that he might have syphilis; to his enormous distress he had learned from the family doctor that his wife had a history of syphilis while she was pregnant with the daughter. He blamed his wife for the handicap and ultimately for the child's death. When the supervisor suggested that the resident pursue the question of blame, and not just loss, the resident was relieved and the clinical picture began to change.

To provide an opportunity for the ventilation of feelings about a patient, and sometimes to invite it, can often have a sustaining effect. Sometimes a patient will generate in a beginner such intense feeling that it is difficult for him to carry on without some opportunity for simple catharsis. It sometimes happens that the work is progressing in a satisfactory way, but that the beginner feels so overwhelmed by the patient's suffering that the apprentice will stumble until he talks over his own distress.

Part of the supervisor's responsibility is to survey the psychotherapeutic material as it develops and to demarcate the various issues that appear. In therapy it may be necessary to help the patient select those areas which he can discuss profitably, avoiding others that may be too overwhelming, and in a similar way it is necessary in supervision to assess the resident's capacity to work with certain questions that the patient may bring up. It is the supervisor's responsibility to assist in the *pacing* of the resident's work, and to exercise judicious influence over what gets discussed, so that neither the resident nor the patient will be overwhelmed. The supervisor tries to avoid issues which in his opinion cannot progress to some satisfactory resolution because of the resident's anxiety. He will try to lead the resident away from certain material on occasion, keeping in mind the optimal direction. He may try to postpone issues, until the resident seems more comfortable. Pacing the treatment in this way can have a sustaining function, because it may prevent the outbreak of disorganizing anxiety and massive avoidance.

The last of the sustaining maneuvers is *actively to ally oneself with the resident's competence,* so that he can proceed with a therapeutic task. A resident may feel so unsure of his capacity to carry an issue through to resolution that he may require this kind of reassurance if he is to continue. Such assistance is frequently needed by beginners who are particularly prone to feel discouraged a few months after commencing their work with psychotic persons. They must be helped over the difficult and sometimes prolonged period in which patients are reconstituting from acute psychotic states. Unless the supervisor is ready to help, in the face of such frustration, a resident may make excessive demands on the patient.

Sometimes a resident may feel quite angry at himself that he is unable to produce rapid, near magical recoveries. On occasion one meets with reactions of acute distress when the supervisor suggests some likely-to-be-helpful step. "But why," the resident will exclaim, "Couldn't I have thought of that myself?" At such moments as these the supervisor should underscore the beginner's potential for learning and hold out the promise of future mastery. "Everyone has to make mistakes," the supervisor sometimes replies. "No one can be criticized for that. The main thing is to learn from misjudgments so that they do not get repeated too many times."

Sometimes a discouraged resident may become preoccupied with prognosis. He may wish to discuss this excessively during the supervisory session, ask the supervisor if the patient can really be helped, if any psychiatrist, even the most skilled, could bring about a helpful change. The supervisor does not on such occasions make any promises, and he may acknowledge the difficulties at hand. But he may also ask the resident, "even though the outcome is uncertain, isn't it worth your while to learn all you can about this kind of patient?"

Supporting Maneuvers

Let us now turn our attention away from the sustaining maneuvers to that second part of the educational armamentarium, the *supporting maneuvers*. The activities which have been described to this point are aimed at keeping up the learner's courage and perseverance in the face of considerable adversity —they help him to stay at his task. In contrast, the supporting maneuvers enable the apprentice to develop his potential for helping patients resolve their difficulties. Without this kind of intervention from the supervisor, a resident will be prone to avoid unsettling aspects of his patient's psychic life, in spite of his best intentions.

Confrontation is one of the major supportive tools. It should be noted at the outset, however, that unless skillfully used, confrontation may arouse excessive distress in the apprentice. For this reason it is particularly important that a strong alliance be built up between the resident and his teacher, marked by mutual commitment to the task at hand, and characterized by respect and trust. Confrontation always involves surprise, and it usually evokes anxiety. The resident is brought face to face with something in his activity with the patient which needs to be altered and unless the proper atmosphere prevails, he may feel criticized, or even somewhat persecuted.

It is because of this that a direct, head-on confrontation is best avoided. Confrontation is necessary, but it must be brought about with tact, not bluntly. Just as "the hardest knife ill used doth lose his edge," excessively abrupt confrontation may stir up resentment and anger that will put the supervisory alliance in peril. Frequently this difficulty can be avoided by telling a story which makes the point or by the judicious use of humor. A good supervisor has a light touch.

One young physician was treating a barber who repeatedly got himself fired from jobs. The supervisor asked if the resident had any understanding of why this was so. When the resident replied, "It is because he is incompetent," it became necessary to deal with his devaluation of the patient. The supervisor first inquired for evidence that the patient was really incompetent. There was none. In this way, the tendency of the resident to project his own sense of professional inadequacy was hinted at but not discussed. It was possible for this irritated apprentice to confront himself with his tendency to devalue. The supervisor was then able to discuss with him how some inquiry into the pattern of job failure might be carried out in a way that would be useful for the patient. The confrontation was carried out, but the resident's tenuous professional self-respect was not unnecessarily battered. Instead, he was shown how to work effectively with the patient and given some help toward his personal transformation into a good psychotherapist who could reasonably be proud of his skill. It was helpful for the physician's self-respect to give up the pattern of devaluation.

Occasionally a resident will report material which is obviously important to the therapeutic task, but he will repeatedly fail to appreciate its meaning. Confrontation is sometimes indicated in these instances.

A resident showed a tendency to dismiss the importance of sexual material which continued to appear in the interviews. The supervisor did not point out this tendency bluntly. Instead, he mentioned, detail by detail, a number of remarks the patient had made over several sessions the implications of which were so obvious that the resident immediately recognized what he had been doing. Although more anxious, he was able to explore this area in subsequent sessions.

A similar technique for confronting is sometimes necessary when a resident distorts what his supervisor has said. It is usually sufficient for the supervisor to review with his resident the details of what has been said in fact on the previous occasion in question. He does not ordinarily need to point out explicitly the distortion and bring about unnecessary embarrassment.

From the pattern of efforts which a supervisee makes to preserve his own equanimity in the face of psychotic material, the supervisor infers what is making the apprentice uncomfortable, and can come to his aid by *sharing some of his own experience.* Avoidances may take the form of oversights, latenesses, or obsessions. In describing how he has in the past managed a similar point in psychotherapy, the supervisor recognizes an avoidance and enables the resident to proceed. Sometimes the supervisor may tell about slips he has made in the past. This will attack the tendency of the resident to fear him as omnipotent, and at the same time offer an opportunity to identify with someone who also has had to learn by making mistakes. A supervisor may sometimes share with the apprentice difficult countertransference reactions which he has experienced and overcome. This kind of supportive maneuver restores the resident's perspective on his competence and holds out the promise for future mastery.

In addition to confrontation and experience sharing, the supervisor may *make clarifications* which will enable the resident to proceed effectively.

> One resident reported a persistent tendency of his patient to attack. Intelligent and perceptive, the patient had discovered that his first-year resident was uncomfortable about his lack of psychiatric experience. He reproached the resident for his lack of experience and depreciated his skill so that the inexperience of the resident served as material for resistance by the patient. The resident, already preoccupied with these matters, felt that his patient had a good reason for complaint, and tacitly went along with the devaluation. The supervisor was able to clarify what was going on; he showed the resident how the patient was attacking in order to avoid certain conflicts of his own. When the resident was distracted from his own preoccupation about professional adequacy and became able to pay attention to what the patient was doing, both resident and patient were relieved and the work could proceed.

Whereas clarification always involves making the preconscious conscious, *interpretation* always refers to comments directed at deeper psychic structures. Interpretation as distinct from clarification may from time to time have a place as a supportive maneuver. The supervisor may detect evidence that his resident has certain inappropriate feelings, attitudes, or expectations about his patient of which he is unaware. Sometimes the supervisor may say something which brings these matters into consciousness. This device is used sparingly, and interpretations are not made about the resident's life outside the therapy he is conducting. There is some risk of the same shock effect that may occur in confrontation, and effective interpretation in the supervisory situation requires a strong alliance.

> In spite of the supervisor's efforts to deal with the problem, a resident permitted a young woman patient to continue scathing, depreciatory attacks in interview after interview. One day the supervisor asked the resident to think whether he had any guilt about the patient or possibly about aggressive women, since it was difficult to understand how he could permit such punishment to continue with so little concern. The apprentice thought the matter over, and though he did not report the details of his associations to the supervisor, he confirmed that the interpretive guess had been correct. Subsequently, he was able to help the patient to investigate her anger at him instead of acting it out with her in the psychotherapeutic sessions.

Occasionally it is necessary to *set limits* with regard to the resident's activity with his patients. Sometimes the resident may continue with some manner of antitherapeutic activity with the patient despite confrontation, sharing of experience, clarification, and even interpretation. In these circumstances the supervisor must awaken in his apprentice some awareness that his psychonoxious conduct is not in accord with his own sense of responsibility and professional purpose. The facing up to this gap between ideals and behavior permits the resident to utilize his own guilt constructively. In most such instances it will subsequently emerge that the apprentice was struggling to avoid some particularly painful aspect of his patient's predicament.

> A middle-aged woman was admitted to the hospital suffering from advanced renal disease with a background of many difficulties and disappointments. At the time of admission the patient was psychotic and faced the probability of death within a year or two. This would mean leaving behind several little children for whom slight provision had been made. It was apparent that her tragic situation and her horror of leaving her children without a mother were important in the precipitation of the psychosis. The therapist was a particularly sensitive and gifted man who made every imaginable objection to this view of the case, minimized the importance of the impending losses, and was almost openly angry at the patient. His supervisor tactfully but firmly reviewed with him just what was going on, concluding his remarks with this statement: "You have your choice between rejecting this patient, or bearing with her through some of this grief. Are you going to treat her or not?" This kind of dealing with the resident would not have been possible without a careful and thorough review of all the material, an attitude of basic respect, and considerable supervisory alliance. The supervisor recognized that the resident was behaving inappropriately with the patient and made the resident aware of the fact. The essential point is that the resident did not know he was inappropriate until the supervisor discovered it and demonstrated it. The resident elected to treat the patient, found it an intensely painful experience, but was able to help her recover from the psychosis.

In some circumstances one must deal with a resident who is unwilling to establish a supervisory alliance, or, at some moment of stress, attempts to abandon it by devaluing his supervisor. There is sometimes a tendency to view the gentlest of teachers as sadistic, or the most skillful as incompetent. This kind of contretemps arises when the apprentice is having difficulty in bearing the frustration psychotherapeutic work entails. "Why do the patients fail to improve? Is someone to blame? Perhaps it is the supervisor's fault." Perhaps some confrontation in the supervision has been particularly painful. The supervisor may then be experienced as brutal. Frequently it is the resident's sense of personal inadequacy and self-contempt stirred up by the beginner's limited capacity to make a therapeutic impact that invites the tendency to see the supervisor as an unfriendly critic.

When the resident begins to miss supervisory sessions, fails repeatedly to bring interview material, involves other supervisors in the case, or otherwise gives evidence of withdrawing from the supervisory alliance, some direct discussion is necessary. Limit-setting in such situations is required. Such a maneuver will define the purpose of the supervisory situation, not as a session for the searching out of sins and the punishments thereof, but as a cooperative effort in which the teacher feels and behaves in a friendly, constructive way toward his junior colleague. Failure to intervene permits the beginner to constrict himself in a narcissistic, self-limiting fashion. He needs to be confronted with his immature effort to devalue a senior who is there with the intent and capacity to be helpful. Such a confrontation conveys the supervisor's conviction that the resident has every potential to learn, and challenges the omnipotent attempt to overestimate his own clinical skill at the expense of someone else. A good supervisor does not permit projection to go unchallenged, although he will avoid excessive abruptness if he wishes to restore the educational effort.

> An able resident reacted sharply one day when his supervisor pointed out a clear blunder in an interview. The resident was clearly chagrined at this, promptly began to defend what he had been doing, and ended his remarks with the suggestion that the supervisor was too quick to criticize and should not assume that he always knew the

best way to proceed. A blunt confrontation was avoided. The supervisor first went back over the pertinent interview material with the resident (confrontation with the *patient* material), and then remarked that he could understand the disappointment at making a mistake of the sort the two were working over together, but he was somewhat surprised at the resident's reaction to its uncovering. With the requisite note of lightness, he reminded the apprentice that in ages past a messenger, bringing a piece of unwelcome news to his king, might get his head chopped off. The supervisor said he felt a little like such a messenger. After a pause the resident said he felt like the king. The two collaborators laughed together, and the alliance was re-established.

Sometimes such tactful handling may not suffice and a greater degree of firmness is required, based always on a careful review of the facts. In some instances it may be necessary to suggest that personal psychotherapy or psychoanalysis for the resident is in order. After extensive supervision and psychotherapy, some beginners will discover that they are most effective in areas of psychiatry other than psychotherapy.

Gratification Maneuvers

There is one final category of supervisory activity, the *gratification maneuvers*. Perhaps the term maneuver is least appropriate here, because so little actual activity is required from the supervisor. The learning is really going on in an almost autonomous way—the apprentice is the active one here, and the supervisor is used as a passive resource. *Validation* is one of these techniques, and *catalysis* is the other.

Psychotherapeutic apprentices can often proceed correctly with patients on the basis of their own understanding and intuition, but they need to review their activity with someone more experienced, in order to confirm that what they are doing is appropriate and useful. All that they need is the supervisor's assent to their creative efforts in helping patients.

A resident once told a patient spontaneously about some particulars of his personal life in a very helpful and appropriate way. In supervision he expressed some doubt about what he had done on the grounds that it seemed rather unconventional. Very little was necessary from the supervisor: he simply said that conventionality was not necessary and that he approved of what had been done. He validated the work of the apprentice.

The term *catalysis* is borrowed from physical chemistry, where it refers to the acceleration of a chemical reaction by some substance which does not directly participate in the reaction, and which may be recovered unchanged at the end of the reaction. There is a parallel in supervision, and the supervisor can correctly be compared to the catalytic substance. Every supervisor has had the happy experience of simply sitting quietly by while a resident is reviewing his work with a patient, and witnessing the moment of discovery when the therapist himself thinks of some useful new way of proceeding or comes on some subtle trend in the material which had previously escaped both supervisor and supervisee. It is the unfolding of the mutual effort in the process of supervision itself which leads to this kind of learning, and the supervisor himself plays an active part in the generation of such new thinking. The apprentice is teaching himself in the context of a constructive relationship.

CONCLUSION

What we have discussed in well-defined categories in this chapter requires much in the way of integration and experience to become meaningful. For the experienced supervisor these perceptions of interferences, defenses, and maneuvers, operate in a moment-to-moment preconscious way. For the beginning supervisor they run the risk of becoming exclusive categorizations or programs of operation, which is in no sense our intent.

We perceive the need for delineation of the intricate pattern of supervision to maximize its impact on the beginning resident.

Many supporting maneuvers will indeed be complicated blendings of clarification and watchful waiting. At times, the question of how much interpretation is warranted must depend on a sense of the strength of the current supervisory alliance. In some instances, the technique of choice will be to clarify rather than expose unconscious reaction formation. The following is a complicated example of the supervisory process as we conceive it.

Early in his residency year, Dr. Roe was enthusiastic in his work with a psychotic Negro man, and in this connection told his supervisor of his own special interest in "social justice" and the problem of racial discrimination. Soon there emerged a repeated, inappropriately authoritarian attitude toward the patient of which Dr. Roe was himself completely unaware. At the same time he unquestioningly took at face value his patient's mildly exaggerated and sarcastic agreeableness. Initially he democratically gave the patient considerable responsibility in deciding his daily dosage of a phenothiazine tranquilizer. After a time, the patient began complaining in a disjointed, psychotic way that puzzled the resident. He said he couldn't trust anyone, he wanted fewer restrictions, and his veins were broken. On further inquiry he said that he was afraid but that the pills were "just wonderful," they made him feel strong and didn't make him "feel flabby at all." On completion of this interview, Dr. Roe abruptly raised and fixed the daily dosage of the tranquilizer without saying anything about it to his patient. On hearing about these developments the supervisor simply discussed with him the patient's curious complaints and exaggerated fondness for the pills. The probability that this was the patient's way of complaining about side effects of the tranquilizer was considered. This was enough to set the resident to reflecting on his management of the case and taking corrective action. The supervisor sensed the countertransference area of interference; the resident's prejudice was ineffectively masked by enthusiasm as part of a characterological reaction formation. Although his arbitrary medication order demonstrated his unconscious wish to control the patient perfunctorily, he was using denial to sustain his reaction formation. The supervisor diagnosed the need for both sustaining and supporting maneuvers. Feeling Dr. Roe could not yet bear confrontation with his use of reaction formation or his actual "social injustice" toward his patient, the supervisor sustained him by purposely refraining from interpreting the matter to him. Support was provided in the form of clarification of the real nature of the patient's communication, and this made possible the correction of mistakes and continuation of psychotherapy. In addition, it was a subtly offered example of the appropriate psychotherapeutic attitude.

The supervisory task requires a high level of investment, attention, and effort from the teacher. Where a supervisory alliance is painstakingly formed, a collaborative effort develops. As the mutual effort achieves its purpose, as the resident can find his own perspective on the lengthy apprenticeship he has begun, the supervisor and resident may have the pleasure of achieving something difficult but valuable. As Spinoza remarked, "All things excellent are as difficult as they are rare." Evaluation of interferences, assessment of defenses, estimation of distress, and supplying sustenance, support, or gratification are each crucial to the work of supervision. In response to these efforts, painstaking and consistent, the uncertain beginner can first experience and later identify with his teacher.

REFERENCES

1. Reich, Annie: On counter-transference. Int. J. Psychoanal. 32: 25–31, 1951.
2. Norton, Janice: Treatment of a dying patient. The Psychoanalytic Study of the Child 18:541–560. New York, International Universities Press, 1963.
3. Freud, Anna: The Ego and the Mechanisms of Defence. New York, International Universities Press, 1946.
4. Bibring, Grete L., Dwyer, Thomas F., Huntington, Dorothy S., and Valenstein, Arthur F.: A study of the psychological processes in pregnancy and of the earliest mother-child relationship. The Psychoanalytic Study of the Child 16:9–72. New York, International Universities Press, 1961.
5. Jacobson, Edith: Denial and repression. J. Amer. Psychoanal. Assn. 5:61–92, 1957.
6. Lewin, Bertram D.: The Psychoanalysis of Elation. New York, W. W. Norton, 1950.
7. Freud, Sigmund: A disturbance of memory on the Acropolis (1936), Standard Edition, Vol. 22. London, Hogarth Press, 1964, pp. 237–248.

CHAPTER VI

Growth and Apprenticeship Learning

By Dan H. Buie, Jr., M.D. and
John T. Maltsberger, M.D.

The ultimate goal of the first year of residency in psychiatry is to initiate successfully a transition from raw beginner to competent specialist. This immensely complicated process can be broken down into objectives and identifications. Obviously, the ability to clarify succinctly and effectively a patient's situation is in part a skill learned by independent trial and error, but it also eventually includes imitations and incorporations of styles demonstrated by teachers. The interchange, the trying out, the working through of such partial identifications give the resident his major opportunity to develop his own professional methods and skills.

OBJECTIVES OF GROWTH

We delineate four overlapping aspects in which we expect to see residents grow: basic attitudes, ego capacities, technical skills, and professional knowledge. Each successive development in any aspect is integrated as the beginner grows to become a mature psychotherapist. A supervisor remains aware of general progress and deficiencies in the course of his experience with a resident, and this awareness is of the utmost importance in the moment to moment work of supervision.

Basic Attitudes

The basic attitudes of a therapist toward his patients are devotion to emotional mastery and growth, respectfulness, and trustworthiness. These attitudes along with the ego capacities detailed below are primary inducements for patients to risk the unknowns of confiding, sharing, and relying on their psychotherapist. His trustworthiness is especially pertinent in relation to his not being exploitative, even covertly, and not being retaliatory.

Ego Capacities

Requisite ego capacities for the therapist are those of bearing intense affects and impulses and those for empathic understanding. A resident's life experience has seldom necessitated withstanding impulses and feelings of the intensity experienced and expressed by psychotic patients. Only by exposing himself to this part of his patient's life and persistently attempting to share it with him will the resident achieve the capacity to tolerate psychic pain. In his attempts to share and understand his patient's emotional experience, a resident may oscillate between a state of transient overidentification with relative loss of reality perspective and a state of utilization of self-protective distancing devices such as denial, rationalization, intellectualization, and viewing the troublesome affect as something foreign to his own experience.

The ego capacity for understanding the patient in the context of his life history, his relationships, and his struggles involves more than the construction of a hypothesis to account for the patient's difficulties. The affective processes of the would-be therapist must be utilized when he imaginatively projects himself into the patient and makes use of the responses evoked in himself for the understanding of the patient. This imaginative projection is *empathy*.* Distinct from sympathy, which implies a noncritical, pitying identification with the patient, empathy makes it possible for the physician to help the patient to understand himself, to bear his pain with less recourse to reality repudiation, to acknowledge his difficulties, to put the events of his life into perspective, and to develop ego-corrective experiences in the therapeutic setting which will lead to more need-satisfying interaction patterns in future dealings with others.

The ultimate foundation of empathic understanding is the psychopathology of the resident's own everyday life, but this is relatively unavailable to the beginner. With experience, perspective is gradually gained, and correctives are obtained on the resident's obscuring projections and introjections. Then he can confidently use his own life in feeling his way into his patient's experiences.

Technical Skills

The skills a resident must acquire center on the diagnosing and the supplying of what a patient needs in order to do his part of the psychotherapy work. For acute psychotic reactions psy-

---

* The word empathy is derived from the Greek *empatheia;* the elements of this word are *em,* in, and *pathos,* suffering or passion. Empathy came into English usage via the German *einfühlung,* and has been alternately defined as "the power of projecting one's personality into, and so fully understanding, the object of contemplation."[1] Empathic understanding involves the critical use of emotions evoked in the physician as he studies his patient's personality and life predicament, and it implies capacity for partial identification with the patient and his difficulties.

chotherapy consists of helping a patient acknowledge, bear, and put into perspective painful external realities. After this is accomplished, work may be directed to correction of the psychosis-vulnerable ego. Diagnoses of these needs are made moment to moment during the interview, and are understood in psychodynamic formulations of what it is the patient cannot now on his own acknowledge or bear, why he cannot, and what he needs in order to be able to do so. Since the capacity for good clinical observation is essential for this effort, the first work with our beginners consists of training in the classical mental status examination, which serves as the foundation for daily patient evaluation, ward management, and decision-making in planning the individual therapeutic programs. This is augmented by additional attention to interactional analysis of the developing relationship between the resident and his patient as has been described by Sullivan[2] and Whitehorn.[3] Reflective history-taking is a learned skill, tending to the eventual apperception of conflict.

Having inferred what the patient needs in order to continue the psychotherapy work at hand, the therapist sets about to supply it. In doing so, he utilizes an acquired repertoire of other skills consisting of helpful activities which we describe as sustaining, supporting, and gratifying maneuvers. Sustaining maneuvers are required when psychic disintegration, overwhelming emotions or impulses, or death itself are imminent. They involve very considerable activity by the therapist, who must do for the patient what the patient cannot do for himself. Examples are supplying external controls, active reality testing, realistic assurance, directives, safety while ventilating intense feelings, and a demonstration of how to bear intense affect by actually bearing it with the patient. Supporting maneuvers require less activity and are designed to help the patient proceed with his psychotherapy work by assisting him in keeping his attention on the painful matters he is inclined to avoid. Examples are confrontation, clarification, interpretation, and limit-setting. Gratifying maneuvers require the least activity. They are of two types. One is catalytic since the therapist supplies himself as an interested but non-interfering agent whose presence merely stimulates and facilitates the patient's doing his psychotherapeutic work. The other gratifying maneuver is the validation of the patient's work, reinforcing his conviction and sense of accomplishment by expressing belief in its solidity.

Professional Knowledge

In addition to basic attitudes, ego capacities, and skills, the resident must also acquire a body of knowledge about psychodynamic psychiatry. To contribute to a clinical approach it must be learned in a clinical setting. The resident attempts to understand each of his patients in terms of a psychodynamic formulation of his life's story. Through his investigation, he learns about the premorbid personality. He discovers strengths and vulnerabilities, assessing this person's characteristic ways of adapting to the vicissitudes of life and of handling emotionally stressful events. The resident puts these data into a conceptual framework of psychopathology in his pursuit of factors which precipitated regression to the extent that this person became a patient.

THE ASPECTS OF THE SUPERVISOR

Supervision is the nurture of positive qualities concurrent with a resolution of interfering ones. The supervisor works closely with the resident, as journeyman and apprentice together, sensitizing the beginner to those tendencies and attitudes in himself which are alienating in effect and psychonoxious to his patients. The supervisor is an experienced psychotherapist who is using customary attitudes, capacities, skills, and knowledge with the resident even though the limited scope of his appropriate teaching function excludes the breadth of inquiry of a treatment situation. But as he goes about his work with his supervisees, the supervisor provides a direct experience of the various aspects of being a therapist. His questions about the affect behind behavior or about the "obvious" reasons for actions are a continual exposure to the constructive interaction of a working relationship. His responses to the resident's patients—and more importantly to the resident himself—are part of an automatic expression of his identity as a psycho-dynamic psychiatrist.

The attitudes of devotion to emotional mastery and growth, respect, and trustworthiness are as essential to effective super-vision as they are to psychotherapy. It might be added that the supervisor must be trustworthy in the same two ways with residents as with patients: he must not be exploitative (e.g., using supervision in pursuit of friendship or admiration) and must not be retaliatory (e.g., returning the inevitable hostility of a resident with punitive or rejecting anger).

The supervisor may be called upon to exercise his own ego capacity for bearing intense feelings and impulses, though it is seldom so intense and never so frequent as in psycho-therapy.

> A resident was trying to remain in the presence of a schiz-ophrenic woman of rapier intellect who seemed capable at any moment of sudden, feline violence. She wore bizarre clothes, including a straw hat trimmed with artificial flowers which was secured to her hair with a long, pointed hat pin. On physical examination, a small, sharp dagger-like letter opener was found concealed in her hair. So overt was the resident's fear that the supervisor felt it trans-mitted throughout his mental and physical being. Bearing the fear was the chief problem the resident was having, and the supervisor spoke of how immediate this woman's threat seemed to him, too. By sharing these feelings with his teacher, the apprentice was supported and could pro-ceed.

A young schizophrenic woman left the hospital and shot herself. For many months, her resident therapist had labored in her behalf, often having to appraise her suicidal potential daily. He had done so on the day she killed herself, and he had misjudged. Shock, fright, helplessness, and despair were the feelings he brought with his announcement. His supervisor, feeling them himself, listened and discussed the reactions as well as touching on the factors leading up to the suicide. In the immediacy of the event, the supervisor gave of himself when he also bore the intense emotions the resident was suffering.

The ego capacity for empathic understanding is continuously operant in supervision. The supervisor automatically feels himself into the experiences of both the resident and the patient he is treating. The capacity for an empathic approach to patients is developed in the context of an empathic reception by the supervisor, and thus the major implement of the psychiatrist can be developed in the apprentice.

A beginning resident was reviewing a difficult situation involving a middle-aged female patient who suffered a combined alcohol-induced neuropathy and hysterical paresis in her lower extremities. In the manner of a *grande dame,* she ordered the nurses to bring her the bed pan and assist her in using it. When they suggested she take herself by wheelchair to the toilet and make use of various supports there to care for her needs under her own power, she became irate and insistent about her weakness. The nurses believed her capable of this and pressured the generally amiable doctor to write orders. He asked the patient about it and then retreated in agreement when she insisted it was impossible. The supervisor told the resident that he could well imagine it was hard to question this lady because doing so meant risking her anger, while the resident preferred to stay in her good graces. Besides, questioning her would involve a review of specific details as to just what she felt she could not negotiate in getting on and off the toilet. Since he knew the resident to be a gentleman, the supervisor suspected he might be embarrassed. The resident knew these things to be true but had not been able to admit them frankly to himself. Having done so, he did take the matter up with the patient, who decided she could, with effort, accomplish her ablutions without further need of nursing assistance.

In the process of applying his skills in supervising, the supervisor is also exercising his clinical skills of observation and investigation, making judgments which discriminate between currently important and unimportant matters, and formulating and testing psychodynamic hypotheses. He strives from moment to moment for psychodynamic understanding of the resident and his interaction with staff, supervisor, and patient. He also tries to formulate in regard to the resident's work his characteristic strengths and tendencies to use particular defensive operations. Knowledge is obviously and openly demonstrated by the supervisor as he verbalizes his concerns, assessments, and questions, bringing to bear the same knowledge of psychodynamic psychiatry used in his clinical practice. His informative discussion of dynamic problems may encourage further pursuit of clinical questions, and he must gauge the resident's current readiness and where appropriate encourage the acquisition of knowledge through literature or seminars.

IDENTIFICATION AND APPRENTICESHIP LEARNING

The practice of psychotherapy cannot be learned from books or lectures. Experience is the primary teacher, and most of the learning arises out of interaction with patients. Only the rarest resident, however, could alone find his way among the snares, pits, and distractions of psychosis without the aid of those who already know how. For this reason, the crux of learning to practice psychotherapy of the psychoses remains the supervised experience of doing it. We have come to consider this learning situation to be an apprenticeship, the resident being an apprentice, the supervisor a journeyman or master.

This apprenticeship relies heavily upon trial and error experience with patients. Insofar as possible, learning grows out of this, the apprentice's own experience. The journeyman or master teacher supplements, modifies, or interferes with it only to the minimum necessary extent. He never does for the apprentice what the apprentice can do for himself, even though the apprentice at times wishes for much more and feels deprived and angry when this is withheld. The supervisor knows that doing more would be at the price of the resident's growth. Inactivity is one of our most important techniques. Teaching of this type is highly individualized, carefully adapted to the needs and potential of each resident, and ultimately directed towards the resident's realizing his particular potential as fully as possible.

The apprentice resident learns not only by clinical experience supplemented by his supervisor, but also by means of the process of identification with his supervisor. In part, identification may begin as conscious imitation, but ultimately it is an unconscious process by which aspects of the supervisor come to be integral parts of the resident's professional personality. The question arises, then, as to which aspects of the supervisor are used for growth by identification. One group of them are those seen in the supervisor when he directly makes available his example of being a psychotherapist for a particular patient. This happens when he shows the resident how to talk with a patient, for example; or perhaps he tells the resident how to do it, or suggests a way to proceed by using an example from his own practice. However, of much greater importance are those characteristics of the supervisor's professional personality which the resident experiences himself in the process of being supervised, for in the course of the supervision relationship the resident experiences in the supervisor all the qualities which he must himself offer to his patients. We consider this to be the most essential element in teaching and learning psychotherapy, and all the supervisor's efforts are designed to serve the goal of being an optimal professional figure for identification. As was mentioned in a previous chapter, the resident has several supervisors, each with attributes, areas of expertness, and points of view individual to himself. Each supervisor is available as an object for identification and is used as such by the resident to whatever degree is personally appropriate.

To restate the concept central to our formulation of apprenticeship learning of psychotherapy of the psychoses: the qualities necessary in the supervisor are those necessary in a psychotherapist, and the resident learns in supervision primarily by means of identification with these qualities as he experiences them in the course of being supervised. The first part of this concept, concerning the identity of the qualities of a supervisor and a psychotherapist, is apparent in earlier sections of this chapter. In these sections, the aspects of each were described under four categories—attitudes, ego capacities, skills, and knowledge of psychodynamic psychiatry. In attitude, both must be devoted to personality growth in others and mastery by them of disruptive emotions, and they must be genuinely respectful and trustworthy, i.e., neither exploitative nor retaliatory. Both require ego capacities for bearing intense impulses and feelings and for empathic understanding. Skills required are similar in that both kinds of work involve the diagnosis of what a person needs in order to remain at and carry out a task and the supplying of that which is needed in order to do so. This diagnosis includes in both cases recognition of how the more primitive defense mechanisms, denial and projection, are being used in the service of avoiding the task. Needs are filled by both psychotherapists and supervisors by means of sustaining, supporting, and gratifying maneuvers. And finally, the same working knowledge of psychodynamics is requisite to each.

It is to the second part of our central concept, that concerned with the process of learning by identification, to which we now turn our attention. Being supervised is painful for every resident, especially early in training, because it entails confrontation with his inadequacies, many of which are a part of his own personality. His distress is made more acute by the tacit comparison of himself with his experienced, relatively more able supervisor, who is usually seen as nearly all-capable. We could properly describe the result as a narcissistic injury, one in which his ideal image of himself as possessor of a personality with penetrating insightfulness and curative powers is badly shaken. There follows the threat or actual occurrence of anxiety and a lowering of self-esteem which is felt as depression.

In an effort to master this painful experience, the resident resorts to various attempts at restitution. Borrowing a description of the process in group psychotherapy by Mann,[4] we could designate this phase of the identification process as the *stage of false conformity and competition*. At this time the supervisor is not only a helpful teacher but also a source of pain, and as a source of pain he is also the object of the resident's anger. In order to validate his anger, the resident often uses familiar devices of denial of the supervisor's actual aspects by substituting either projections of his own anger or devalued qualities he wishes he could find in him. Thus he can convince himself that his supervisor has not evidenced certain desirable aspects, or is mean, or is stupid. At the same time, the resident may protect himself by denial of his own incapacity and perhaps even resort to overestimation of himself. He then can consider himself as good as or better than his supervisor, at least in some respects. The anger, denial, projection, devaluation, and overestimation of himself are used in various degrees and combinations. The result is a wide spectrum of possibilities, ranging from avoidance or otherwise completely shutting out the supervisor at one end to a collaborative competition at the other. Where a resident begins on this spectrum and his range of use of it varies with the individual. But most of the time his use of these devices is secret, concealed by an appearance of conformity, or by what amounts to a caricature of his teacher.

The supervisor's part in the identification process is one of maintaining constancy as an object for identification. In the face of covert or overt opposition, which may be persistent, he continues to perform the sustaining, supporting, or gratifying maneuvers repeatedly as the need requires. He stands the ground of his experience, while at the same time allowing the opposition inherent in the phase of false conformity and competition to continue, provided it is compatible with eventual progress and the patient's welfare. He does not respond to the resident's hostility with hostility. To do so would be equivalent to acting out a countertransference in psychotherapy. By conducting himself in this manner, he further serves as an object for identification in that the resident must do much the same with his patients in order to be a good object of identification for them.

As the identification process continues, the first stage gradually and irregularly gives way to the second, the *stage of true conformity*. This stage is summed up in the old adage, "If you can't lick 'em, join 'em." The resident has tested the supervisor long and often and found him good and valuable. He has also learned through experience that his restitutive attempts, his false compliance, and competition, have been unsuccessful by virtue of being unrealistic. They have failed to gain him the progress toward competence that he wants. So he abandons his negativism and joins his supervisor in a true collaborative effort, one which eventuates in a degree of identification with him, such that he finds himself automatically working with his patients in ways he has experienced being worked with by his supervisor. The process is variable from resident to resident: some work through it sooner, some later;

some make extensive identifications, others use it to a minor extent. The process is an unconscious one, and the professional identifications thus made proceed to operate in an automatic, unconscious way. Growth is not confined to the boundaries of supervisory hours, and once set in motion the whole identification process will continue long after formal supervision has terminated.

REFERENCES

1. Onions, C. T., (Ed.): The Shorter Oxford English Dictionary. Oxford, Oxford University Press, 1959.
2. Sullivan, Harry Stack: The Psychiatric Interview. New York, W. W. Norton, 1954.
3. Whitehorn, John C.: Guide to interviewing and clinical personality study. Arch. Neurol. Psychiat. 52:197–216, 1944.
4. Mann, James: Psychoanalytic observations regarding conformity in groups. Int. J. Group Psychother. 12:3–13, 1962.

CHAPTER VII

The Supervisor's Rewards

By Julius Silberger, Jr., M.D.

In previous chapters, we have described our understanding of what the experience of psychosis means to the patient and a therapeutic framework within which the patient can be helped to deal with his conflicts in a more integrated and realistic way. We have examined the problems of the beginning psychiatric resident as he is faced with his own internal hindrances to learning about psychotic illness, and how he can bring himself into a helpful alliance with his patient. Having outlined the areas of interference and maneuvers of avoidance mobilized in the resident, we have discussed the techniques by which the supervisor can try to help him not to retreat from the learning situation. The more positive aspects of learning by identification of pupil with teacher have been considered, and it now remains for us to consider the supervisor himself and the rewards for his teaching.

By experience and by testimony one knows that this kind of psychiatric teaching sometimes seems as slow and as repetitious as the work of the tides. To persevere in it must testify either to awesome dullness of spirit or to complexity and intensity of purpose. Although the supervisor will usually have had a better opportunity than either the patient or the resident to understand his own motivations, he is still likely to take for granted or to ignore some important aspects of his inner drives. His failure to recognize the urges underlying his own manifest behavior can in part reflect an understandable reluctance to acknowledge in a public way what he may see as very private feelings. It is our experience that his hesitation reflects not only his discretion but also certain unconscious wishes: wishes to avoid facing the selfishness of one's own impulses, or wishes to preserve inviolate the cherished fantasy that one's own motives are *so* unique that they do not apply to others, to the common run of one's colleagues, so that undergoing the discomfort of clarifying them may offer, at best, merely personal information, but nothing of broader reference.

But *many* psychiatrists find the opportunity to teach psychiatric residents attractive, and even allowing for the uniqueness of their individual motivations, there is enough of commonality of purpose to nourish the hope of finding some general trends, and there is enough need to understand the supervisor's motivations to justify setting aside these hesitations. If we try to describe in detail what we feel are the immediate satisfactions and the more devious hopes which this work nourishes, it is because we are convinced that many of these hopes, which spring from irrational and contradictory impulses, can interfere with the effective learning and practice of supervision itself and make harder what is already a hard enough job.

The members of our workshop are, for the most part, young in their experience, and for that reason particularly susceptible to and aware of certain aspects of "becoming" teachers, as contrasted with "being" teachers. In some part, our interest in the work of supervision stems from the hesitations and uncertainties we found in our own experience of becoming supervisors, and we are more likely to be particularly aware of those aspects which reflect our own developmental struggles, and which are in this way analogous to what we have described for the beginning resident and indeed for the patient himself.

For one raised in the medical and psychiatric tradition, becoming a supervisor has much of the feeling of a professional "rite of passage." It comes at a time of increasing independence and responsibility and brings the opportunity to maintain a tie with the institution in which one has grown up but now in a new relationship. This excuse to hold on to the mother institution is particularly important at the onset of one's independent career because of the feeling that one's training is not yet assimilated into a wholly coherent clinical style. The concept of apprenticeship learning implies a progression to journeyman at the end of residency, and some of the uncertainties of the role of the supervisor motivating our workshop spring from the ill-defined process of growth between journeyman-therapist and master-teacher.

As a step in the development of professional integration, a young psychiatrist after finishing his residency will be noted to pour his energy into a process of active mourning over the loss of his training experience, his colleagues, his patients, his old habits of thought. He struggles with the need to defend the orthodoxy of his past from the challenges of new situations, composing sober, perhaps maudlin or even outraged evaluations of what he has learned and where he has been short-changed in his training. Gradually he can look at the old place with new eyes, deploring or applauding the inevitable changes and feeling the differences within himself as he gives himself the time and the clinical opportunity to grow new objectives and new perspectives. This mourning process occurs whether he goes away or stays close to home and seems to depend more on internal needs than on external circumstances.

During the residency period and in the years immediately after, trainees follow their own individual interests and personality styles by tending to move into research, administration and community consultation, or clinical practice and clinical teaching. Of course many, perhaps most, maintain some investment in more than one of these three kinds of activity, but each of them can become absorbing, demanding a different way of organizing and employing one's time and one's thoughts. The man who goes into clinical practice often feels that he is isolated in his office, particularly in contrast to the complex relationships he experienced as a resident in training. To balance his feeling of professional loneliness, he uses those institutions which draw strength from their attention to this particular need: the professional societies and study groups. He may also use less appropriate avenues of consolation: he may turn social occasions into opportunities for shoptalk, threatening his own sense of discretion, boring his friends, and bringing his hostess to despair. Thus, even aside from the actual occasions for teaching which it provides, the teaching institution serves his other needs. It offers him a forum for discussing his ideas, a chance to expose himself to the criticism and pointed questions of colleagues and students, the occasion for lunch with a friend, the opportunity to rethink the obvious. This adventitious compensation of the part-time teaching appointment is so highly valued that many clinicians will set aside for it extra hours from an already burdened schedule.

Other rewards which are also peripheral to the actual experience of teaching are the opportunities to participate in selecting candidates for residency (one's future colleagues) and sometimes the occasion to nourish and sustain an academic interest or scholarly ambition. The maintenance of a teaching appointment at a medical school has a competitive value among colleagues as well as a personal gratification upon becoming a member of a faculty alongside one's former teachers. As more hospital appointments become full-time ones, the need remains to recruit for the teaching program from among those whose primary interest is in clinical practice. In psychiatry more than in other fields the boundaries between clinical practice and basic research overlap, and the experience of the one stimulates the hypothesis-formations of the other.

One might object that these concerns have little to do with the actual experience of being a supervisor, and yet, because they are so important to a clinician's career and pleasure in doing his work, and because they are so relevant to basic aspects of the structure, staffing, and effectiveness of the training program, they must be considered seriously and respectfully.

But let us leave now these secondary gains of the supervisor and turn to a consideration of his more primary rewards and conflicts—those of his association with his supervisees. The general objectives are: for the resident, the development of independent capacity in the effective diagnosis, understanding and treatment of his patients; and for the supervisor, the knowledge and feeling that he is participating in an important association with his student.

In any relationship between two people, conflicts and motives may be awakened in each, at all levels of psychic development, and these may appear to sidetrack the supervisory relationship. In this sense, there are obvious parallels between the supervisor-student pair and the student with his patient, and there is similarly an analogous experiment in learning being undertaken by the supervisor, resident, and patient. Ideally, the resident serves as a resource for the patient's self-understanding, and draws his support from the supervisor, who in turn serves as a resource of conscious awareness for what is going on inside of and between all the various parties to this complicated undertaking. Each individual comes with very personal, often unrealistic, expectations, which may be in conflict with the actual accomplishment of his purpose. Each approaches his goal by learning to tolerate the experience of confronting impossible wishes and enduring their frustration in the hope of accomplishing some ideal purpose. There are specific kinds of irrational conflicts and motivations to which the supervisor seems to be particularly susceptible, some of relatively greater weight at the outset of one's career, others of continuing difficulty.

In his own personal and professional insecurity, the supervisor may overly encourage the resident in his tendency to idealize his teacher; or he may resent unduly the resident's need to reject everything the supervisor has to offer. As discussed in connection with areas of interference, either reaction fails to perceive the resident's own learning problem. Professional maturity has been said to consist in large part of increasing comfort in the awareness of one's own ignorance. Perhaps judicious respect for the limits of one's ignorance carries implicitly an equally just appreciation of the extent of what one does know. In any event, a young supervisor is particularly prone to exaggerate one or the other. Tending to lead him astray, to smother his humility and to make him defend his self-assurance, are the alternating tendencies of the resident to overidealize his teacher, on the one hand, and to project onto his teacher the resident's own sense of frustration and incompetence. Idealization can be pleasant music to the supervisor, but it carries the underlying message that the resident despairs of his own capacity to develop his own understanding and style. The beginner may feel hopeless about developing a personal and valid approach and adopt some prefabricated technique from his supervisor.

The obverse side of this tendency, that of rebellion, is the position which the resident might take, that to bring a detailed account of his transactions with the patient into his supervision would be to enslave himself to the supervisor's control, that the supervisor has led him astray, anyway, because he tried what the supervisor "told" him to do and it did not work, so that it is all hopeless. Or that he has read of a radically different method, or that he will devise something of his own and not be beholden. To the degree that the supervisor himself is moved by anxious uncertainties about his own limitations and capacities, he will be susceptible to misreading and mishandling such provocations.

A second series of situations arises from the tendency and capacity of the supervisor to identify with his student, remembering how it was when he was a beginning resident. Certain advantages accrue to the resident, particularly in the interest and sensitiveness of the supervisor, qualities which the supervisor enjoys finding in himself as well. Empathic understanding of the resident must be checked from becoming indulgence. Indeed, the very intensity of the supervisor's investment is likely to distract him from a few very special problems of his job. One is the resident's natural tendency to bring into supervision his own personal issues, which are awakened or intensified by the range of stimuli intrinsic to close work with severely disturbed patients. Remembering how uncomfortable his own early experiences were, the supervisor is likely to be particularly sensitive to the resident's problems. Because of his own clinical orientation and his sympathy, he may be tempted to respond in clinical ways as a therapist but without the resources of time and therapeutic contract which would be available in a real treatment situation. The supervisor must limit his own participation to the structure imposed by the bounds of his relationship with the student, that of a teacher who is concerned about his student's difficulties in learning a specific task, and who has at the same time a certain responsibility to share what he knows and to attempt to facilitate the best possible treatment of the patient.

The further question of how much responsibility the supervisor has for the patient is also complicated. As our hospital is organized, responsibility for the patient resides primarily with the chief of the ward service to which the patient and the resident are assigned. The supervisor may have no direct connection with that service, and whether the supervisor should even see, much less interview, the patient is a matter of some controversy: we feel that this depends most appropriately on the resident's needs, which are met through supervisory maneuvers, as indicated in the last chapter. Even more, the degree to which the supervisor becomes actively involved with the administration of the patient varies, and may vary in response to the supervisor's wish to take over for himself some of the resident's responsibility and some of that of the service administrator. Such intervention is rarely successful, stemming from dubious motives, arousing the resentment of the resident and of those others in more direct contact with the patient's situation and with more responsibility for it. It seems to proceed from a mixture of motives, but obvious among them is competition, often masquerading as the wish to save the resident from failure, embarrassment, or self-doubt. One can even discern a patronizing disguise for some resentment which the supervisor feels for his apprentice and which he is reluctant to acknowledge to himself.

Another aspect of identification and its pitfalls stems from the supervisor's unquiet memory of his struggles with some of his own supervisors when he was a resident. He may try to become the supervisor he himself would have wanted, rather than the resource his student may need. His earlier wishes may have reflected irrational facets of his own particular character structure, which he, by implication, is now imposing blindly on his student. The inevitable cost is mutual resentment, resentment from the constrained student as well as from the rebuffed supervisor, the latter feeling that his "best" efforts are unappreciated.

The quality of being dissatisfied with one's own experience and being determined to rectify this for the coming generation is among the most powerful motives for those who become teachers of medicine. Although this may be true for all teachers, it is particularly important for physicians whose choice of medicine itself as a career reflects their style of dealing with pain and danger by learning to control them and channel their use with therapeutic intent.

Even the other less hostile and more ideal identifications, with teachers from whom one has learned gratefully and the emulation of whom may bring the most intense pleasures of teaching, may evoke difficulty in the learning situation insofar as the supervisor imposes on his resident the undigested inspiration of his own experience. The resident picks and chooses from this treasury of inherited riches only those few peripheral crumbs which happen to suit him at the moment. It is the burden of those who wish to pass on an intact legacy to know that their independent heirs will most surely dissipate their inheritance according to their own whims and circumstances. But one unanticipated dividend may come from attending to those unresolved aspects of experiences with one's own teachers. Very much like the experience of those who while struggling with the daily facts of parenthood gradually come to a more harmonious relationship with their own parents, one may become more able to recognize how much of the difficulties of the past were at least in part a consequence of one's own irrational demands, and how impossible is the demand for and the expectation of perfection. And how well one can make do with less than that.

Indeed, making do with less is not only possible but even necessary if the student is to develop an independent capacity. If the supervisor were ever to achieve unmitigated perfection as a resource (whether as an expression of his pleasure in showing off to a captive audience, or in the need to preserve a position of *noblesse oblige,* or even from sheer benevolence) he would find that he had inhibited the resident by supporting his tendency to depreciate his own developing capacities. There is little danger of such an ideal disaster: even if the teacher were ready, certainly the student would not be. The possibility is as available in some form as are all of the other syndromes of overprotection and has a similar emotional rooting.

Another expression of this controlling and protecting tendency, now allied to the inevitable pain of parting, is the supervisor's wish to hold on to his students. Aware that in the year of their work together, the job of learning and teaching can never be accomplished, the teacher may be discouraged at always beginning a job but never enjoying the pleasure of completion, even leading him to doubt the practical usefulness of his work. The recurring experience of losing his students, the yearly mourning of the departed, may blunt the freshness of his involvement and may lead him to resent his new students, seeing them as unsatisfactory replacements for their predecessors, less intelligent or less well motivated, or less respectful or appreciative. In this respect, the man who teaches a limited and defined curriculum is fortunate in having a final examination which he can look back on to console himself for the loss of his pupils. At least, if they have gone, he can feel satisfied that they learned something concrete. Working with problems of emotional learning is unending for the student, as it is for the teacher, and the proofs of accomplishment are rarely tangible.

In summary, then, just as happens in other aspects of personal development, becoming increasingly skilled as a supervisor requires modification and sublimation of the supervisor's more primitive wishes in the attempt to achieve a more complex purpose. This is a task never fully done, no more for the supervisor than for the resident or the resident's patient, and the decision of any of them to continue in the struggle must reflect the assessment that there is something in it for each that makes it worth his while.

Appendix

In 1962, Semrad requested 150 teachers of psychiatry to answer a questionnaire surveying their experience and attitudes. One hundred responses were received, the majority (92) from the Harvard Medical School Teaching Services.

The respondents ranged in age from 27 to 56. The largest number felt that their guiding educational philosophy was psychoanalytic or psychodynamic, primarily, but strongly influenced by sociological and biological ideas. Most spent an appreciable part of their time in general clinical psychiatric practice and in psychoanalysis, with a fair proportion, though in diminishing numbers, in administrative psychiatry, child psychiatry, clinical research, basic research, and the psychiatric study and treatment of special conditions. A very few of those responding spent small amounts of time in neurology, the study of mental retardation, and public health. It is clear that if these questions had been asked today, 6 years later, there would be some shift of numbers into the last category, public health, which would now be expanded to include community psychiatry, but the sample would not be very much different in other respects, and is, with these reservations, quite homogeneous.

The larger part, by about two to one, felt that residents in their first year should have primarily inpatient experience, with a greater emphasis on outpatient experience in the second year, and the introduction of subspecialities mostly after the second year. Similarly, the large majority felt that the resident's personal psychotherapy or psychoanalysis was an appropriate and important part of his training experience. These attitudes perhaps reflect the organization and values of the teaching services from which the respondents were drawn.

116

They were asked to rate and compare in importance the ways in which teachers might contribute to a resident's difficulties in learning. Two factors were singled out as particularly significant: (1) the teacher not understanding or disregarding the learning processes of a resident, and (2) the teacher's overloaded schedule not permitting fulfillment of his desire to teach. Four other factors were also felt to be of significant importance, although in diminishing degree: (1) situations in which a teacher was inadequately prepared for a given assignment, (2) the difficulties imposed by a teacher's theoretic prejudices and/or value conflicts, (3) a teacher's loss of desire to teach, and (4) poor emotional health of teachers. Such matters as, (1) frustrations of teachers apropos the low status of teachers compared to that of researchers or administrators, (2) problems of teachers being part-time, and (3) the complications of physical ill health were felt to be of little significance. Indeed, some respondents made a point of doubting that teachers really are of low status in the teaching situation, compared with their colleagues in research and in administration.

Questions were then asked to evaluate what were considered the most common causes of a resident's difficulties in his own learning. Among these, the resident's neurosis was generally felt to be a serious factor, followed by inadequate preparation and time for reflection, overloaded schedules, neurotic choice of vocation, and the temptation to slight one's training to make money (and the implied need to do so). Of lesser importance were felt to be such factors as value conflicts, disappointments at nonacceptance to various career positions, economic burdens, self-overprotection, resentment of authoritative teacher attitudes and administrative structures, and uncertainties aroused by clashing viewpoints among staff members. Again, problems of physical health were felt rarely to be significant.

Teacher techniques were rated; as one might expect from

the composition of the responding sample, problems-oriented, case-oriented, and resident participation teaching opportunities were most highly valued, reflecting either the philosophy or the experience that learning by example, sharing of common experience, and interest stimulated by practical need and by active participation are the most effective stimuli to learning.

An attempt was made, without success, to distinguish among schematic teaching processes in terms of their relative importance. For example, the teacher serves variously as a resource of clinical information, of clinical skill, of clarifying operations, of security-giving operation, or of help in dealing with other hospital and community personnel. Although there was tendency in the questionnaires to acknowledge particularly the importance of the teacher as a source of security, the schema did not evoke other distinctions. Similarly, attempts to separate out specific factors in the residents' relations to other people in their lives, their families and neighbors, non-psychiatric colleagues, mental health groups or agencies, religious groups, and to see if the teacher had a special place in helping residents with any of these in any significant way brought no significant correlations and did not evoke much interest in the respondents.

Finally, although teachers generally value free expression, awareness of one's own limitations, reality testing, and introspection and place less emphasis on such operations in the teaching situation as giving active help, these values generally parallel those implicit in dynamic psychotherapy and in psychoanalysis.

In summary, what this questionnaire succeeded in doing was to outline the general assumptions of our own academic community, point to some of the generally recognized practical problem areas, and emphasize again that the questionnaire technique samples only the surface derivatives of inner feelings and deeper motivations, which themselves do not yield except to a more personal and painstaking investigation.

Index